THE
KENT
COLLEGE
CENTENARY
BOOK

THE
KENT
COLLEGE
CENTENARY
BOOK

Christopher Wright

B.T. Batsford Ltd, London

Acknowledgment

The author and publishers would like to thank the following people and organisations for their permission to reproduce the photographs listed: Martin Cox (57, 68 and the colour photographs on the back and front jacket); David Currey (60); Christopher Dickinson (67); Kentish Gazette (47, 48, 49, 51, 52, 54, 56, 59, 61, 64); Pictorial Press (53).

ISBN 0 7134 4777 X (cased)

Typeset by Tek-Art Ltd, Kent
and printed in Great Britain by
Anchor Brendon Ltd,
Tiptree, Essex
for the publishers
B.T. Batsford Ltd.
4 Fitzhardinge Street
London W1H 0AH

Contents

Contents

List of Illustrations

Black and white photographs

Frontispiece   The original drawing and plan of the school

Introduction

Now that I have completed this *Centenary Book*, I am left with a vague feeling of loss. Ever since the Governors asked me to compile some impressions of Kent College's first hundred years I have felt myself to be living with large numbers of men and women, dead and alive, who have worked at the school. I have pictured them going about their business in the same buildings as those in which I have been working for the past 15 years, and being elated, depressed or frustrated by similar experiences. Now that the job is over, I can only thank the many contributors who have responded to my requests for help so generously and have written, either for publication or for my own use, their memories of their time at the school. They have clothed and shaped the dummies of the past which would otherwise have been lifeless.

A long list of those to whom I am indebted would be out of place, but two men, in particular, demand mention. Adrian Slater has helped me continually. Scarcely a day has passed, particularly during the past year, without our discussing a point which has arisen, or without his unearthing some new fact or piece of information. He has compiled a statistical record of the school's development which is being printed separately and can be obtained from K.C. I hope those who are interested in our story will read it, and that they will also try to obtain a copy of the *Jubilee Book: Kent College 1885-1935* (Kent County Newspapers Ltd., 1937). I have quoted freely from this collection of memories of the school during its first 50 years, but the whole book should be enjoyed.

Finally, I want to thank Professor Barker of the London School of Economics, until recently a Governor of Kent College, for reading my typescript and making detailed and constructive comments on it.

Christopher Wright
May, 1984

11

CHAPTER ONE

Early days (1885-8)

It all seems to have started with extraordinarily little fuss. In 1883 the Reverend Benjamin Browne, Chairman of the Directors of the Kent Wesleyan Methodist Schools Association, read a Memorandum of Association to his fellow directors. It was proposed to

> . . . establish and carry on in the county of Kent (and elsewhere if expedient) day and boarding schools for boys and girls in which there shall be given at a moderate cost a sound education, combined with moral and religious training on the principles of the Wesleyan Methodist Connexion, as set forth in the first four volumes of sermons of the Reverend John Wesley and in his notes on the new Testament, and in which no religious doctrine shall be taught contrary thereto.
>
> In particular to establish immediately, and carry on at or near Canterbury, one such school for boys – and to establish and carry on at Folkestone one such school for girls.
>
> And to obtain for the shareholders dividends at the rate of £5 per cent per annum on their paid-up capital in the Company . . .

A house called Hoathe Court opposite modern Kent College, a hundred yards back from the Canterbury-Whitstable Road and a mile and a half west-north-west of Canterbury, was purchased. The date of the opening was fixed for Tuesday, 20 January, 1885. On Monday, 19 January the first two boarders arrived – Elfick and Scott (aged 11 and 15 respectively) and three others – Hewson, Hine, and J. Hobbs (aged 11, 9 and 14) – came the following day. Three day-boys – the brothers Baker and Alec Rennie (aged 11, 13 and 12) – joined them. K.C. had started.

The Directors were taking part in a general movement among Methodist clergy and laymen of the time to promote secondary, or what was revealingly called middle class, education throughout the country. Truro School had been founded by a group of local Methodist shareholders in 1880. In the next year the East Anglian Wesleyan School Association established the East Anglian School at Bury St. Edmund's (now Culford School). The Kent Colleges at Canterbury and Folkestone were part of the same movement. Each school had to rely for income on fees paid by its parents and for capital on private shareholders. There was no money to be had from endowments nor, so far as I can discover, from benefactors – apart from the gift of the land on which modern K.C. stands (*see p. 16-17*) – nor from the Methodist Conference, nor from the local authority – let alone the Board of Education, and this shortage of capital for even the smallest expansion handicapped K.C. from the beginning of its history. Indeed, it is quite extraordinary that it survived its early years at all.

The first headmaster of Kent College was James Deaville who had been Head of Woodhouse Grove School in Yorkshire, then the Junior School for Kingswood School, Bath, from 1875 to 1883. He was described as a man of:

> an unusual type; broad shouldered, slightly corpulent with an easy springing walk; a leonine head; hair slightly curly at the ends and over the ears; massive moustache and heavy beard of a somewhat golden fairness. His eyes were kindly, but when necessary could flash with anger. He would have made a great Viking in appearance at any time. (Louis Elworthy in *The Jubilee Book*: Kent College 1885-1935, Kent County Newspapers Ltd., 1937, p. 4)

We are fortunate in having a memoir of those early years written by one of the founder boys whose names I have just recorded, F. Hewson. It appeared by instalments in the first numbers of the *K.C. Magazine* (1891) and was reproduced in full in the *Jubilee Book*, pp. 1-29. I can only reproduce a few extracts here, and would urge all those who are interested to read the memoir in full, for it is a litle gem:

> Hoathe Court in summer was most delightful to live in. My first thought when I came along the drive to the front door was: 'What a pretty place!'; my second: 'But it is a school after all.' Soon, however, we all got to like the place very well. There was a lawn in front of the house, a garden on one side, and a playground behind, overlooking the farm-yard of Hoathe Court. On one side there was a little orchard, and round this some land planted with shrubs, having also some very high trees in it. This plantation, as it was called, was never swept or weeded, but was quite wild, and often we used to stir up a hare or a rabbit; these animals came out of the wood on the other side of the field. There were also squirrels here, which we often saw, but never caught, nor did we catch either hare or rabbit. The picturesque surrounding of the neighbourhood made us like it all the more,

Kent College, Canterbury,

Report for the Term ending *April 22nd* 1887

SCHOOL REPORT.

Name *S. Pittock*

Subjects of Study.	Details of Work.	Form.	Number in Form.	Average Rank.	† Mark for Diligence.	Master's Name.
Religious Knowledge	I Kings 12 – II Kings 16.	IV C.	12	1.	1.	Arthur Scott B.A.
Greek	Exams.	„	„	3	1.	B. Glanville B.A.
Latin	Allen's Latin Grammar — Rudimenta Latina	„	11	9	1.	A.S.
French	Contanseau's Academic Chardenal's Exercises De Vigny's "Canne de Jone"	„	11	3	1.	A.S.
German	Weekly Problem Paper.	„	14	1	1.	A.S.
Mathematics	Arithmetic Areas, Interest, Discounts Algebra Multipl. Division, Factors, Simp. Eqns. Problems, H.C.F. Euclid I 1-9	„	14 / 14	5 / 8	1. / 1.	A.S.
Science	Rain, Snow, Winds &c.	„	—	—	1	B. Glanville B.A.
History	Collier's British History 1066 – 1399	„	13	1.	1.	A.S.
Geography	Gill's Smaller Geography. England.	„	13	1.	1.	A.S.
English Literature and Grammar	Morris English Grammar. Shakesp. Mids. Night's Dream. Dictation Analysis & Parsing	„	15	10	1.	A.S.
Writing	Copy Book.				1	A.S.
Drawing	Freehand				1	A.S.
Music	Piano. / Singing (Sol fa)				1	H. A. Fricker B.

* The School is divided into Forms, of which the VIth is the highest.

† For Diligence, 1 is the highest mark, —6 is the lowest.

Average Rank in Form this Term _2_ Good Conduct Marks ‡ this Term _201_ Out of _220_

DOMESTIC REPORT. Good Conduct Marks ‡ this Term _216_ Out of _220_

I cannot speak too highly of Sidney's work this Term. The improvement has been most marked.

Jno. Glanville B.A. Head Master.

‡ Each boy is credited with Twenty marks per week, one or more of which may be lost for misconduct of any kind.

Next Term begins _Friday May 6th_

School report: A.S. must have been a teacher of many parts

especially as at the beginning we used to have the run of the whole place.

The house itself was a very good specimen of an old English country-house, with a fairly large hall, two good sitting-rooms, one used as a dining-room, the other as the Headmaster's study, a large scullery and kitchen, etc. Some men were making a well in the kitchen on the day we first came. Upstairs were bedrooms of different sizes. On the following day, Tuesday, the next boys appeared. They were Hewson, Hine and J. Hobbs . . .

Our mode of life was simple and home-like; we all sat at one table, Mr. Deaville at one end and Mrs. Whyte (the Matron) at the other, and for the first week or so we had Mr. and Mrs. Browne and Mr. Scanes to dine with us. They took the greatest pains to have everything good and sound. After a few days our number was increased by the coming of another fellow, Larkin. Our school order was fixed by an examination and Scott earned the distinction of being the first head boy.

We received great kindness at the hands of Mr. Chapman [the neighbouring farmer], who allowed us to go all over his place just as we liked. The gate of the farm-yard adjoined our play-ground, and there was another little door leading from his farm-yard into our garden. This door was constantly being left open, probably by the farm lads, and the pigs consequently were often in the garden. This was rather a nuisance, especially if we were at the time all in school hard at work. Nothing remained but to drive them out again as quickly as possible, but pigs, however, are not easy things to drive; they seem always to go in exactly the contrary direction to that in which you wish them; so that much time was often lost before they could be induced to return to their native land . . .

When we had been open a year we became too numerous to live all in one house, and were divided into three companies. The majority of us stayed at Hoathe Court under Mr McOwan, some went down to 35 St Thomas' Terrace[1] to sleep, and a few (about five or six) went over to the Court House[2], which was then occupied by Mr. Drayton. Those of us who went down to the Terrace numbered about fifteen . . .

We had a holiday one day at the beginning of the summer term, 1886; one of the old-fashioned holidays, which are scarcely known now[3], when masters and boys, high and low, monitors and plebians, all go off for the day with the sole intention of having a good time of it together. It was a glorious day, warm and sunny with just a gentle breeze, and we made for Whitstable. Beyond an interview with an agriculturist who was moved to anger because we climbed over a hedge, nothing very eventful happened on our way out. When we arrived at Whitstable we procured two boats and some of us went for a sail. We had a delightful time, but the fishermen didn't get a very miraculous draught of fishes.

The main reason why K.C. was able to move so easily from Hoathe Court to its present site was the generosity of one Mr. Edward Pillow, whose name was later commemorated at K.C. in the form of the mysterious 'Pillow Prize'. Edward Pillow, a member of a Canterbury

Huguenot family, was a farmer who lived at the farmhouse of Neal's Place[4]. He gave the school five and a quarter acres of land on which to establish itself[5] a stroke of great good fortune. Plans for the erection of the main building now went ahead and are recalled by Hewson:

The great event of the summer term 1886 was the Stone Laying of the new College. A large number of parents and Directors were present at the ceremony. As the day was hot and there was little wind, we boys standing in the full blaze of the sun were most unpleasantly warm. The stone which everyone has seen in the hall was laid by Horace Brookes Marshall, Esq., J.P. Lunch was provided for the guests in a tent which he had erected on the lawn the evening before. The speeches were good but to our minds it seemed that the lunch was far better, and we fear our affections are so set on things earthly that we still remember the lamb and green peas . . .

About Easter 1887 the new buildings were ready for our reception. From living a species of pleasant, happy family life, we were to pass to the sterner reality of public school life. The first thing to do on moving day was to get our books and other small belongings across to the new school. This we did, the first thing in the morning, and then had the remainder of the day to ourselves. We all went off to Whitstable to enjoy the balmy breezes of the briny ocean, and after a long day's enjoyment and a sumptuous tea, we left this town of oysters and returned to our new quarters refreshed and greatly elated by the day's events. On returning at seven o'clock, we found ourselves installed in the new building: to Hoathe Court we had bidden a final farewell. Masters, boys and all alike then set to work to carry bed-irons, mattresses and bed clothes upstairs. It was not till after half-past ten that we were able to retire for the night . . .

After a rather heavy fall of snow at the commencement of the spring term, 1888, snow-balling was much in vogue, and for several days we had snow-fights with the C.O.S.[6] boys, in which our masters assisted us by making ammunition for us. One object of the fights was to capture as many of our opponents' caps as possible – symbolising scalps, I suppose. For a few days the battles were fought in the open road, and we quite held our own. At length, the C.O.S. boys, aided by some agriculturists of the baser sort, and armed with wooden shields, made a fierce onslaught on our gate. Mr. Young, during an interval of peace, came out and went forward to effect an exchange of caps: they took the opportunity of very unchivalrously giving him a volley of snowballs and otherwise insulting him. Bad blood being thus imported into the struggle, the fights were strictly prohibited . . .

At the end of the summer term, 1888, Mr Deaville held an assembly in the schoolroom. He congratulated us on having come to the end of another very successful term, and wished us a very pleasant holiday, but he had something to say which it would give him a great deal of pain to say. When we returned we should probably see someone else in his place as Headmaster. He expressed the greatest sorrow at having to leave, but he felt that, owing to decline in health, he could not successfully discharge the duties which his position in the school required, and that he could not conscientiously stay with us any longer. He went on to say that, when he thought of the old house over the road, the small number with which we started our career, the great success we had had so far in every way, and how we had become a well-known school in east Kent, he could not express the sorrow he felt at having to leave us. He hoped that we should go on as we had begun and have continual success, and that after his trip abroad, he might be able occasionally to come up the hill and have a look at us and find some who would know him and welcome him as an old friend. This was his parting address; we were all completely taken aback by the unexpected and unwelcome news.

Mr. Deaville must have recovered from his illness, for next year he went to Rydal as Second Master and stayed there until his death 20 years later.

CHAPTER TWO

K.C. (1888-97)

James Deaville's successor was a Cambridge graduate L.W. Posnett, previously senior mathematics master at the Leys School. Posnett, like his predecessor, inspired fear. (It seems to have been a requirement of headmasters of this period. One can imagine the decisive intervention at the Directors' meeting called to appoint the new Head: 'Yes, yes, gentlemen. Robinson is a good enough man in all conscience but he doesn't inspire *fear*. Now Mr. Posnett is a very different man . . . .)' But he also inspired respect and affection.

Posnett played in the football and cricket elevens with the boys, though with no particular distinction. Like all heads of small schools he seems to have done his fair share of teaching, particularly of the Bible. So far as we can tell he was securely settled at K.C. when a dramatic episode ended his headmastership. One of his pupils, W.O. Roberts, writing 50 years later in the *Jubilee Book* (pp. 44-7) recalled it:

All schools have their ups and downs, their good boys, bad boys, heroes and bullies. It was regrettable that we had a band of the last-named – the only incident that upset, for a time, our happy school life. There were two boys who commenced what was known to us as a bullying club; these two gradually inveigled others into their net, until the number was eight. They themselves called it the C.H.W.B. Club, these being the initial letters of the surnames of the first four. Their methods were unjust and unkind, and their victims nearly always the smallest boys. Their process was to invite youngsters to one of the classrooms and to hold a mock trial on most trivial accusations. Invariably the poor lads were found guilty. They were then birched with willow twigs purloined from neighbouring trees. I remember to this day the misery and fear to which some of those lads were subjected, but I must say that some of those eight bullies took part in this vile practice against their own conscience and inclination. One of these in particular told me how dreadful it was to him and how he hated it, but feared for himself if he broke away from the rest of them: he was the smallest boy of the eight. This unhappy state of affairs went on for part of two terms; eventually the headmaster discovered it and instituted an inquiry. I was then getting into the Upper School, as we called it, and was one of about a dozen or so who was sent for by the head to his study and questioned; he wanted to know if I had ever taken part in it and requested the names of those who were the bullies and those whom I knew to have been victims. He saw my hesitation and told me that I need not fear these boys, and that it was his determination to stamp out this practice. This gave me courage and I told him everything I knew, feeling that the misery at the school was at an end.

The Headmaster did not act hastily; it was obvious for days afterwards that he was worried and anxious, not in his usual bright spirits. I am sure that during those days he was giving a great deal of thought and consideration to what his action should be in the matter. Several days after I had been to his study, we were all in our various forms, and suddenly we were given the order to close books and cease work; books closed, we were told to assemble in the dining-room in our usual seats. The assistant masters came in and stood at the front of the hall; a few seconds later they were followed by the Headmaster, looking very pale (he usually had a florid complexion) and carrying with him two canes. The eight boys were called from their seats and stood, as directed, beside the assistant masters. Then with tremulous voice the headmaster addressed the school. I cannot remember his exact words, but the substance of his speech was of an apologetic nature, and the expression of his sorrow to those youngsters who had been subjected to the misery. Then, turning to the eight guilty ones, he told them they had been guilty of a vile practice, and by their reprehensible deeds had made the lives of these lads unhappy, and that he had decided to administer to them punishment which he hoped they would never forget; they got it – twelve to fifteen strokes for each of them, well and truly delivered. How happy we all were that night! No invitations were issued for mock trials or canings; those unhappy practices ceased for ever.

But this was not the end of trouble; the parents of those boys who had been punished by the Head were advised that their sons were no longer required in the school for reasons which were explained to them. Some of them did not approve. Later there was a meeting of the directors of the school, where the subject was discussed. Naturally we did not know anything of their deliberations, but it culminated in the Headmaster's sending in his resignation.

Today, remembering the fear, misery, and unhappiness caused in the school at that time, I am still, and always have been, of the opinion that the Head was justified in his action. He later opened a private school at Broadstairs, and evidently many felt that he was right, for two of our assistant masters and several of the boys went to his new school.

He was succeeded by Mr. J. Smallpage, who had been High Master of the York Castle High School, Jamaica, for the last five years. The school Smallpage took over in September 1893 was more of an all-age coaching establishment than a school, though all who remember it talk of its warm school spirit. There were 51 boys, of whom eight were day-boys. Their ages of entry ranged from eight to 16, with 11, 12, and 13 the most common. Most left when they were aged 14 to 16. Many spent two years or less at K.C. Half of the 51 came from Kent, and ten from London. Four of the boys were sons of clergy, presumably Methodist ministers.

Mr. Smallpage's reputation as a man keenly interested in all sports and games had preceded him. Those who hoped he would live up to it were not disappointed as Roberts' memoir (pp. 47-8 of the Jubilee Book) makes clear:

Smallpage was small in stature: several of us in the upper school were taller than he. With his advent there were many changes in the school routine and new assistant masters, and with these latter there were quite a number of changes in a short period, though I forget the order in which they came and went; their names were Kitto, Pickles, Trotter, Goodfellow, Shelton, Habbut.

Mr. Smallpage, having lived in the tropics, introduced something of tropical methods with regard to school hours. It is customary in hot countries to have a siesta in the afternoon. We did not work, but we had no siesta – we played. The afternoons were taken up with sport, and in place of afternoon school, we had an hour's work before breakfast, half-an-hour extra tacked on to morning school and the same to evening prep.

Punishments in the Smallpage regime became healthier. There was a larger roller for the school pitch, usually horse-drawn; the horse, which had been hired from Fleury, a neighbouring farmer, went into abeyance, and we boys supplanted equine labour. Instead of a master shouting at one, 'Brown, 100 lines,' it became, 'Brown, ten minutes' rolling.' This was supervised by a master, so we had to 'pull our weight'. In addition to being a healthy punishment, another advantage accrued – with the exception of the St. Lawrence county ground there was no better pitch within miles of the school.

Smallpage's headmastership seems to have developed the vigorous, manly, out-door ethos which breathes from the pages of the school magazine. Games, cross-country runs, country walks, a knowledge of natural history, a type of 'muscular' Christianity, respect for missionaries, evening concert parties and entertainments often arranged at very short notice – all these were encouraged by the Smallpages. They must have run a warm, friendly ship. Yet, after a while, there are signs that all was not well with the régime.

To begin with, there was the basic problem of numbers of boys on the books. By the time Mr. Smallpage left at the end of 1897 there were only 32 boys in the school, although as his first Prospectus stated:

the buildings . . . afford comfortable accommodation for about 100 boarders . . . special attention is given to the domestic arrangements; the dormitories are large and well arranged; each boy has a separate bed provided with a spring mattress; there are good lavatories . . .

In September 1895 the Chairman of the Directors, Mr. John Holden J.P., of Folkestone, had expressed the wish that parents would soon be sending them a greater number of pupils. After all, he pointed out, Kent College at Folkestone – the predecessor of Kent College, Pembury – had 100 girls. Then there was the rapid turnover of staff, which Roberts remembers. Old Boys complained in February 1895 that 'the teaching staff is almost entirely changed and the very rules of the school are different from those which we once thought it our duty to try and dodge.' In Smallpage's last term the Magazine refers to staff changes as an 'exodus'. There was also the standard of school work. It is true that the Magazine makes regular reference to the boys' entry to examinations conducted by the College of Preceptors. But one Prize Day Mr Smallpage revealed his priorities. He spoke at length about the value of compulsory games, and praised the growth in 'honesty, straightforwardness and manliness' which contributed to the 'good, moral tone' which had been established in the school. For examinations, however, he had little time:

> During the year the boys had gone in for but few exams. In many cases the parents were not anxious that they should do so and he sympathised with those who considered that exams were a great deal overdone in these days.
> (*Kent College Magazine*, 1897)

Even if Smallpage and his staff had longed for academic excellence, there was little they could have done about it. A glance through Smallpage's entry book with its entries in stiff, upright writing inscribed by a scratchy pen, tells us something about the varied standards with which he had to cope. He admitted 28 boys, for instance, in 1894 whose ages ranged from eight to 19. Of these, one-third stayed for two years or less. There must also have been continual financial worry. The school was in trouble in June 1892 and the Directors were allowed two more years in which to repay a loan while they tried to raise a further £2000 worth of shares to meet their obligations.

For whatever reasons Mr. Smallpage left K.C. at the end of the Christmas term, 1897. Mr. F.M. Facer, who had been teaching at Woodhouse Grove since 1886, succeeded him. He was the fourth headmaster to be appointed in 13 years.

CHAPTER THREE

K.C. in the 1890s
as seen through the eyes of the
Kent College Magazine (1891-7)

K.C. had been in existence for six years, and had 50 boys on its books, when the first copy of the *Kent College Magazine* appeared in April 1891, price 6 pence. Fig. 4 shows a print of the main block of the school, as seen from the junction of Whitstable Road with Giles Lane, in a faded mixture of fawns and greys, captioned 'Wesleyan College, Canterbury'. The block looks very much as it does today, nearly 100 years later, but a study of the Magazine, which had its origin 'entirely in the monitors' room', according to its first editorial, reveals a world as far removed from the K.C. of the 1980s as the diaries of Samuel Pepys. It was a simple, straightforward, manly world where virtues and vices were clearly defined, and the possibility of a grey area in between the two was never even suspected.

Many of the Magazine's pages are taken up with the affairs of the Debating Society. The Society started in October 1890, at first met weekly, and claimed an average attendance of 25. In November it came down firmly on the side of total abstinence. In February next year it passed a vote of censure upon Russia for her persecution of the Jews, but at the same time expressed a wish that 'no more Jews might be imported into England'. A week later it tried the Secretary for the unsatisfactory discharge of his duties and found him guilty. On Easter Saturday the motion that the 'opening of museums on Sundays was injurious to public morals and calculated to bring into England the continental Sunday' was defeated by one vote, while a discussion on capital punishment reached no apparent conclusion.

A large proportion of the Magazine's pages were concerned with sport. Though some of the matches were for boys only, members of staff played regularly with the boys in many cricket and football elevens, contributing three members of the cricket XI in 1891, and four of the football team. (No thought of rugby intrudes into the editors' world.) More village and club sides were played at cricket then than now. There were plenty of cricket matches, and the eleven travelled as far afield as Folkestone for a game. The eleven clearly owed a great deal to Mr. Ingram, who made 1000 runs during the 1894 season in 24 innings at an average of 70, and took 72 wickets. (In the previous season he averaged 54 with the bat, while the next player averaged 7.5). K.C.'s general cricketing record was good. But they must have had a traumatic experience at Ramsgate, where they played St. Augustine's College, on 29 May 1891, and were dismissed for nought. The writer in the Magazine was less than generous about this remarkable feat:

> In four overs and four balls we were all dismissed for no runs at all, not even a bye. Howley, no doubt, was a splendid bowler, but it is no exaggeration to say that the wicket was fully accountable for half the destruction for it was on a slope and full of holes. The balls broke right across the wicket, bounced right up over the wicketkeeper's head, or shot straight along the ground . . . . Scarcely one of our fellows escaped without being damaged in some way or other, Webster indeed had a very serious blow in the face.

The wicket seemed to recover, however, sufficiently quickly for St. Augustine's to make 117 on it. They then dismissed K.C. again for 50, to win by an innings and 67 runs.

Relations with St Augustine's appear regularly to have had their problems, for in the 1895 match the Magazine's cricket reporter comments sourly, 'This match should certainly rank as a win, as our opponents, after only losing five of their wickets for 39 runs, refused to continue play on account of the light'.

The first entry about football makes clear that the general principle of voluntary participation in sport caused trouble from the beginning, as it was bound to do in a school of 50 boys, destined to fall to as little as 32 within a few years.

By the summer of 1894 compulsory sport was the order of the day. This was clearly the wish of the new Headmaster, Mr Smallpage, who disliked boys who 'sat around the reading and school rooms' on whole holidays rather than taking a ten-mile walk. With the coming of compulsory sport – and on three afternoons a week – something of the original family atmosphere, which was clearly the essence of the Hoathe Court years, had vanished, never to return. Less time was spent exploring the unspoilt countryside which stretched from the K.C. gates to the Thames Estuary, or roaming Blean Woods. Only nine years earlier football had been a game, prompted by impulse to fill the needs of the moment, and played by those who enjoyed it on a lawn about 25 yards long, from which the ball would sail over the hedge, or obstinately lodge in a tree.

In the 1890s three whole holidays were regularly given each term. They were given at short notice by the Headmaster, and the day was chosen because the weather prospects seemed good. The practice started with paper-chases. One anonymous writer had no doubt that the most important feature of a good whole holiday was 'the fodder'. He and his friend would order a meal for three – he loved a good beef-steak, as supplied by the Carlo Maestrani Restaurant in Sandgate Road, Folkestone – and tuck in:

> I am not a believer in spending a whole day off without having a good square meal in the middle of it. If you have only an odd sandwich or two, or a few biscuits, there is a gnawing and chafing sensation inside, which tends to affect your temper, so that you become silent, and if not silent, snappish . . . . The moral I have drawn from my experience of whole holidays is that if you wish to spend a whole day in love and charity with your companion, you must have a good dinner.

On summer Sunday evenings, the boys walked back from their second compulsory attendance of the day at the Methodist Church in Canterbury by way of the footpath across the fields which then covered St Thomas' Hill. This proved a particularly fruitful time for the collection of frogs, newts, toads, slow-worms, and lizards. These were kept, in the usual schoolboy way, in bottles stored in lockers, or in matchboxes carried in the worshipper's pocket, and formed, in one writer's heavy words, 'a rival attraction for the captivator's attention with the more profitable words of the preacher'.

It was, however, the collection of butterflies and moths from Blean or Church Woods for which K.C. boys were peculiarly well situated, then as now:

> Canterbury and its surroundings, the Church Woods in particular, are capital hunting-grounds for butterfly and moth collectors, and not unfrequently the keen entomologist would return on a hot summer afternoon, late for school, and bathed in perspiration, but jubilant in the possession of some hitherto unattained trophy, a Green Hair-Streak or a rare Fritillary. Cockchafers, or May-bugs, were plentiful in the summer and we used to vie with each other in catching these on our return from chapel after the Sunday evening service, by the more pleasant route through the fields. Some will remember the creepy sensations they once experienced on feeling the repulsive clinging of one of these insects on their toes . . . .

Some years later Virginia Woolf who was renting Moat House, then the property of Mr le Fevre, of the Canterbury Huguenot family, had a less happy experience of the moths from Blean Woods. In a letter to Saxon Sydney-Turner, in June 1910, she writes:

The rain falls, and the birds never give over singing, and hot sulphur fumes rise from the valleys, and the red cow in the field roars for her calf . . . I pick chocolates out of a box and worry my sister. Shortly before the rain began, three days ago, we had our windows prized open by a smith. The decay of centuries had sealed them. No human force can now shut them. Thus we sit exposed to wind and wet by day, and by night we are invaded by flocks of white moths. They frizzle in the candles, and crawl up my skirt to die in the hollow of my knee. There is something unspeakably repugnant in the feel of creatures who have lost their legs.(*Virginia Woolf*, Quentin Bell, vol. 1, p. 162.)

Evening concerts – often arranged at very short notice after the boys returned from a whole holiday – seem to have been a regular and much loved feature of K.C. life. All that the Magazine tells us about them is in keeping with the general manly ethos of the times, and conjures up a picture of boaters slanted at exagerrated angles, of hands on expanding chests as soloists take off to reach their crescendoes, while accompanying pianists strive desperately to keep pace. Mr. Smallpage and his wife seem to have been particularly fond of these occasions, and at the end of the first whole holiday of their reign we read: 'Mrs. Smallpage sang two pretty songs, "Wishes and Fishes" and "Home Dearie, Home". Mr. Smallpage sang, and also recited "How Bill Adams won the Battle of Waterloo", while Mr. Goodfellow sang "Anchered".'

Christianity – or rather a particular type of Methodist Christianity – breathes from the pages of the *Kent College Magazine*. Well-supported Bible reading societies, Christian Fellowship meetings, talks by returned missionaries, worship twice each Sunday at St. Peter's Methodist Church in Canterbury – these are as much part of the boys' lives as sport, or work, or evening entertainment. An entry in the Magazine for February 1895 catches the tone: 'From October 14th to October 23rd the Reverend T. Waugh was in Canterbury engaged in Evangelistic Work. On 18 October he gave us a Special Address in our Dining Hall. His remarks and advice were very plain and to the point. He said that serving God did not make a milksop of a boy . . . .' The school's religious faith was part of its general ethos – to be a Christian was to be a decent fellow. That the code of the decent fellow might contain un-Christian beliefs was a proposition which was never mentioned in the pages of the Magazine.

CHAPTER FOUR

K.C. during Frank Facer's headmastership (1898-1911)

In headmastering, as in politics, the winner takes all. Teachers, like politicians, may protest at the injustice of this rough and ready rule. They may point to circumstances beyond the control of any headmaster. Independent schools are directly affected by the rise and fall of middle-class incomes. The skill and devotion shown by members of staff whom the Head inherits may have more influence on the school's life, than the character of the Head. But little notice is taken of such subtleties. Schools, particularly small family schools like Kent College, are generally believed to succeed or fail because of the quality of their Heads.

Certainly there was no contemporary hesitation in attributing praise for the change that came over K.C.'s fortunes after Mr. Facer's appointment. He himself set the tone. At his first Prize Day in July 1898 his words were blunt enough, one would have thought, to make Mr. Smallpage consult his solicitor: 'In January he found the work at a very low ebb; many boys had left and the masters were strangers to the remainder . . . . As to numbers, he found in January 32 boarders returning. There were now 46 boarders and three day boys.' (*Kent College Magazine*, 1898)

When, over 13 years later, he retired to become a priest in the Church of England – he was Rector of Shepherdswell near Dover for many years – the article in the Magazine commemorating these years told the same story:

> Those who are aware of the lamentable state the place was in when he took over the direction of affairs are best able to appreciate his great services to the school. At that time . . . it was an insignificant institution and very little was known about it that redounded to its credit. The buildings were small and very inadequately equipped, the numbers low, and the general tone poor. The task of remedying these gross defects promised to be an

unenviable one, yet by dint of consistent effort in the face of great difficulties it was successfully accomplished and now one can truthfully affirm that everything is changed. The buildings are large and up to date, . . . the numbers have been at times over a hundred and the tone is distinctly high.

The new head took up his appointment at the age of 35 – a well-built, vigorous-looking man, to judge from his photographs. It is easy to imagine him striding purposefully across the school fields to join the little crowd watching a match by the charming, pagoda-like cricket pavilion, built during his time from subscriptions by Old Boys, to which he himself had handsomely contributed. Or one can imagine him, architect and builder in his wake, pacing the outline of the new school room, soon to be built as a gesture of confidence in the Head by the school's Directors. He had been born at Stratford-upon-Avon in 1863 and had been educated at Stratford-upon-Avon Grammar School. At 16 he had, in the manner of those days, joined the staff of 'a middle class school' in Birmingham without any qualifications and, in 1882, had joined the staff of the Wesleyan College, Truro (now Truro School). In 1886 he went to Woodhouse Grove School, where he became Second Master. His salary was described many years later by his daughter as 'infamous' and he was expected to act as Bursar on top of his many teaching commitments. At Truro he had become a local preacher and circuit steward of the local Methodist church. He studied to take a Bachelor of Arts degree at London University, which he gained in 1893. One consequence of his time at Woodhouse Grove was the appointment to his staff of J.T. Hargreaves at a salary of £60 a year with board and lodging. Hargreaves had been a pupil at the Grove in Facer's time. He stayed at K.C. for the next 35 years and when he retired wrote of his old Headmaster:

Mr. Facer undoubtedly laid the foundations of K.C. as we know it now. In 1898, when he came, there were about thirty boys in the school, but in a few years the numbers rose to over a hundred, and during his time the greater part of what is now K.C. was built. Mr. Facer was strict – yes, but he was no tyrant. He was really a most lovable man, and, like most kind men, his sternness was really the result of his love . . . .

Mr. Facer was a deeply religious man, and, great Headmaster though he was, I think that he found his real mission in life when, on retiring from K.C., he entered the Church. When he was Headmaster his sternness always seemed to be his most striking feature – it may have been his rather fierce moustache that gave him that expression – but when I visited him at his rectory at Shepherdswell, his face seemed to radiate mellowed kindness, and I don't think that the change was entirely due to the absence of the moustache. The combination of these two men was to me, who knew him so well, the real Frankie Facer.

His memorial in the school hall says that he lived what he taught. No truer thing can be said about him than this. I remember seeing him in 1918, when he had just heard that his son had been 'reported missing'. He spoke to me so calmly about it, and about its being in God's hands. 'After all,' he said, 'I am one of God's ministers, and can I honestly talk to my people about trust in God if we (he always coupled his wife with himself) don't trust God ourselves?' 'He felt what he said: he lived what he taught.' Can a finer tribute be paid to any man?" (*Jubilee Book* pp. 111-13)

Others write along similar lines. The late A.L. Horrell (K.C. 1910-15) refers to Facer as an 'introvert', who was succeeded by the 'extrovert' Brownscombe. Mr. Percy Goble (K.C. 1902-6) refers to him as 'big, dignified and moustachioed'. The late H.W. Skinner (K.C. 1910-17) arrived to board at K.C. on his eighth birthday, never having been away from home before.

My main feeling was fright. I remember Mr. Facer as being very grave and austere in manner. The only personal thing I remember is being taken out into the playing field with other small boys and strung out in a line while Mr. Facer would hit a golf ball down the line and we had to find it and return it. This, as I remember, is the only sport he indulged in.

From the beginning, Frank Facer had clear ideas about the sort of school over which he wanted to preside. These ideas seem to have remained basically the same throughout his period of office and he applied himself loyally to them throughout his 13 years. He seems to have lived much more closely to the boys than does a modern headmaster, and his name is constantly appearing as taking part in debates, or a mock trial, or an end of term concert. He placed great emphasis on school societies – the Choral and Literary Societies, for instance, to which he added the Debating Society, of whose importance he was convinced. Drill, carpentry – he sensibly employed the local carpenter to teach the boys his craft – gymnastics, Bible classes, a Natural History Society – all these were to flourish in Facer's K.C., as indeed many of them had done in the K.C. of the 'nineties.

The outside world occasionally invaded the world of the *Kent College Magazine* (renamed for some reason the *Rampant* in 1906), but only in the form of royal deaths or wars. Its tone remained the same as it did in the 'nineties. (Was the copy compulsorily submitted for censorship, one wonders?) The boys were forever grateful to the staff, for their efforts on their behalf, and rarely did a hint of criticism enter the Magazine's pages. The mass picnic continued to be rapturously applauded, year by year. The usual venue was Herne Bay, and, in the Facers' first summer, the whole school drove through the woods in three of the largest breaks in Canterbury, arriving in time for a bathe before lunch. They returned at dusk accompanied by 'tin trumpets, mouth organs etc.' to K.C. where 'after singing God Save the Queen and giving three cheers for Mr. and Mrs. Facer we ended a most delightful day. . . . . Perhaps never before had the weather been so ideal, the arrangements so perfect, the goodwill and kindliness of everyone . . . so absolute and inspiring.'

Shortly after Facer's arrival, the Directors advertised their confidence in him by launching a considerable building programme. By the summer of 1900 the editor of the Magazine is writing:

> We hardly know ourselves, with a handsome Gothic schoolroom, capable of accommodating three hundred people, five large classrooms, spacious lavatories, a cloak room, tuckbox room, library, covered play-shed, two fives courts [what became of them I wonder, and why were they allowed to fade away?], asphalt playground, new dormitories, a large changing room, hobby room, prefects room, and dark room.

The total cost was around £6000. The accommodation of this 'middle class boarding school', as the Prospectus still described K.C., was suitable for 120 boys, though boarding numbers never reached that figure in Facer's time. Two years later a new art room was opened, and the art master, Mr. Curnow, who was to stay seven years – far longer than most of his colleagues – had started taking sketching walks in the area round about the school.

Much of school life was still conducted in the open air. A cycling club was formed in 1901, and members used often to cycle to the sea. Greenfinches nested in a bush at the front of the school. A nest of young larks was found near the tennis courts, by bushes in which nightingales sang for a fortnight in June. Facer presented a sedgewarbler's nest to the Beaney Museum in Canterbury. The Magazine noted the large numbers of boys who kept silkworms, which were fed mainly on lettuce, while in 1907 Old Boys and others planted 51 trees on the edges of the school fields. (Pupils of a more recent date will remember Dr. Sangster's similar tree-planting morning in the summer of 1980.)

In 1905 the school was advertised as having seven resident and five non-resident staff, though many of the latter were part-time teachers. The staff was, no doubt, like Facer himself at Woodhouse Grove, miserably paid, and, to our modern eyes poorly qualified. Hardly any were honours' graduates, though some achieved further qualifications by correspondence. Most were unmarried, and many were birds of passage. But they worked long hours, and were faced with discipline problems at least as daunting as those which confront their successors in the 1980s. It obviously helped if you were a 'manly fellow' – i.e., a games player. In

1900, before the President of the Methodist Conference, Facer claimed that 'all our masters are Methodists and three are local preachers.'

Although the numbers had increased so strikingly – in 1901 the Chairman of Directors was commending the school's firm financial condition on Prize Day 'to the consideration of any who might be thinking of investing in the few unsold shares' – the basic educational weaknesses of the school remained the same. These were caused by the nature of the intake: the boys' ages ranged from eight to 18, few stayed past 16, and many still stayed for only two years or less. Using the Kent College entry book, which Facer compiled in his own firm, clear hand, and taking 25 boys who entered K.C. in 1905, together with another 25 entering in 1908, I found the following facts. Of the 50 who entered:

> 2 boys were aged 8
> 4 boys were aged 9
> 2 boys were aged 10
> 6 boys were aged 11
> 6 boys were aged 12
> 7 boys were aged 13
> 13 boys were aged 14
> 5 boys were aged 15
> 2 boys were aged 16
> 2 boys were aged 17
> 0 boys were aged 18
> 1 boy was aged 19
> —
> 50

Of these 50 boys:

> 10 spent 1 year or less
> 8 spent 1-2 years
> 22 spent 2-3 years
> 4 spent 3-4 years
> 4 spent 4-5 years
> 2 spent over 5 years
> —
> 50

Twenty-six came from Kent, Sussex, and Surrey, 16 from elsewhere in the United Kingdom (though none from Ireland) and eight from abroad; three were sons of clergy.

It is not very surprising that during these years Facer was heard complaining on Prize Day that 'so few boys remained at school sufficiently long to have much impression made on them. So few stayed over 16 that the higher exams were, as a rule, out of the question.' Facer's own son, Geoffrey, won a scholarship to Mill Hill in 1910, after six years at K.C. and his exact contemporary L.G. Atkins transferred to the Leys, Cambridge, at the same time. J.C. Hosking (K.C. 1899-1905) completed his education at University College School, as his memoir, reproduced on p. 36, shows.

Sport continued to take up a third or so of the pages in the Magazine. In 1903 John Hargreaves started his long association with school sport. Under his care the First XI cricket square was to maintain its quality and to develop into a first class batting wicket, well known in the county, and remembered as such by Mr. Godfrey Evans (K.C. 1929-36), when he returned to K.C. to open the new scoreboard in 1982. Mr. Evans attributed its quality to the hours of rolling put in daily by John Hargreaves, assisted, as often as not, by boys in detention – a practice started, as we have seen, by Mr. Smallpage. Football continued to flourish. Hockey was introduced in the Easter term, as was fives and shooting, with a school rifle corps.

At the beginning of the autumn term in 1907 Frank Facer, after ten years at K.C., announced his forthcoming resignation, only to take it back again within a few weeks. The Directors, and no doubt others in the school community, who knew that at 45 their Head had much life remaining in him, persuaded him to stay on. Two years later the Matron, Miss Hicks, who had come with the Facers, having previously been Matron for six years at K.C. Folkestone, resigned and was presented with the sizeable leaving present of £110. She was respected and remembered affectionately by generations of Old Canterburians. The next autumn, as we have seen, Geoffrey Facer transferred to Mill Hill. The school was still developing all the time: a large 'physical laboratory' was opened in 1908 and the school went over to a house system in 1910 (Red, White and Blue houses under housemasters Hamblen, Claypole and Hargreaves respectively). There were the usual school boys' crazes – diabolo, kite-flying, roller-skating. Dandies were to be found everywhere, some flaunting 'gorgeous brown brogues', others 'delicately tinted rainbow socks' and others again 'a magnificent expanse of white waistcoat'. A head of 'finely groomed hair parted with mathematical precision' brought its owner great respect.

It must, however, be recorded that when the Facers finally left in April, 1911, closing the school early because of German measles, numbers had fallen to 68 boarders. It may be that the drop has little significance. With a change of headmaster boarding numbers soon reached 100, and they might have done so if the Facers had stayed. But the fall occurred at a time when there were more successful middle-class families than ever before and more children were attending boarding schools[7]. Perhaps there was

1 Hoathe Court: it all began here

2 James Deaville – The first headmaster

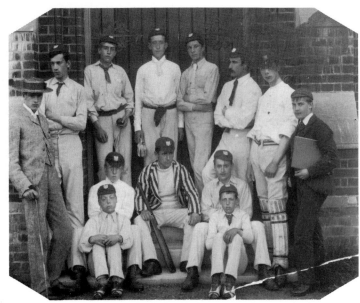

3 1890 cricket XI. *From left to right:*
(back row) P. Tice (umpire), C. Allen, P.W. Wacher,
E.C. Hobbs, F.L.S. Riggal, L.L. Wilkes Esq.,
A. Hobbs, G.L.C. Graham (scorer);
(middle row) W.T. Cox, C.H. Simpson Esq.,
H.A. Fricker Esq., *(front row)* I. Capeling,
C.H. Hagger

4 *Kent College Magazine* – Number 1

SCENES FROM THE FACER PERIOD

Frank Facer, Headmaster 1898-1911

6 Facer on Prize Day, July 1902, with his daughter

Edwardian Bloods

8 A form group

9 and 10 The school sets off on a whole holiday

11 K.C. football 1906 – something of a staff XI

Mr. Monahan. Mr. Harris. A. Walker. J. E. Parker. A. V. Leighton. G. A. Catt. D. de Koningh.
Mr Knock. Mr Hargreaves. R. G. Beard (Capt) Mr Hamblen. Mr Claypole.
A. Stevens E. N Brooker.

12 The school room. Note the gas lighting, the basis of many practical jokes

13 Alfred Brownscombe,
Headmaster 1911-34

14 Old Boys' Weekend before the First World War,
with both the new and the previous Head and their wives

15 Kent College Cadet Corps 1915

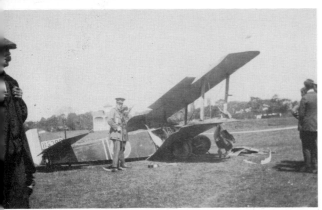

16 'A service aeroplane crashed on the cricket field ... one summer morning while the school was at breakfast.' (Memories of Geoffrey Brownscombe)

17 Another landed on the same day, 21st May 1918

18 and 19 Scouting started at K.C. during
the First World War. The troop's founder
was a woman teacher, Miss Phare, pictured here

less drive from the top. Perhaps Frank Facer should have stuck to his original decision and resigned in 1907. The fact remains, however, that it was he who, in his first ten years, saved K.C., and then laid the foundations of the modern school, using materials of the soundest quality.

CHAPTER FIVE

Memories of K.C. during the Facer period

Childhood memories of K.C.: 1900-11

Written in 1978 by Margaret E. Moyle, daughter of Frank Facer

To have any kind of picture of life at K.C. in those distant years, one should realise the complete absence of motor transport, and the consequent quietness. If one needed to go to Canterbury, one walked both ways, as I did when I was six, to a small school in the Dover Road and as my mother did for shopping. The only transport was provided by an ancient, Pickwickian-like, small coach, run by Solly and Vane and drawn by two horses. It started from St. Dunstan's, through the city for one penny, carrying six passengers whose feet were kept warm by thick straw. I can't see Solly and Vane getting rich quick – or ever!

But to return to the school. On the domestic side there was no trained person, as I am sure there is now. My mother, with experience only of a small home and one maid, undertook the supervision of 16 maids and a cook of mature years, whose husband lurked in an evil smelling dungeon under the back stairs, where he stoked the boiler and, I think, cleaned boots. My mother also ordered meals, dealt with shops and a store room, and of course acted as hostess, as headmaster's wives did and still do. (I now have a daughter in that position[8].) Did she, I wonder, keep the accounts? I am pretty sure she did not, but, then, who did?

The health of the boys was looked after by a dear old apple-cheeked Cornish woman, Miss Hicks, (to me 'Hickie' and a best friend). She had, however, no training and depended entirely on common sense, kindness and castor oil, with reference if necessary to old Dr. Wacher. What happened if there was an epidemic and many boys needed nursing I don't know, but I think a nurse was called in – I certainly hope so.

Later on, I remember the arrival of a Matron, Miss Haton – you can imagine what the boys did with that name. She must, I suppose, have succeeded Hickie, who got too old, but her reign was short, and even a nine-year-old knew why, but a 78-year-old is not telling.

34

I knew the names of all the boys. While they filed in to dinner my father and mother and I used to stand in the hall, at the bottom of the stairs, and then follow on to the top table, where we sat in company with about eight or nine masters. I can remember the masters' faces and voices, but only two names – Mr. Claypole and John Hargreaves. My father, poor man, carved for all at the top table, but how food arrived on the boys' plates, or whether it was good, I do not know.

On Sunday there was a procession to Chapel in Canterbury. I expect the Methodist Chapel is still there, it was a solid building. It was packed in those days, especially during term time. The procession was composed of solid blocks of boys about six deep each way, in the charge of a master and, as there was never any traffic, they marched unhindered in the middle of the road. Honesty compels me to record the intolerable boredom of these services. Wearisome, long extempore prayers (I was mercifully allowed to kneel backwards with elbows on the seat, so I just went to sleep), and a sermon not infrequently over an hour. Poor boys, seated sideways under the eye of the Headmaster – no sleep for them.

The Minister was Mason Penn, and it was his youngest daughter, Fanny, who became my governess. There had been several unsuccessful holders of that office, but as soon as dear 'Penny' entered the nursery, my brother and I knew she had to be obeyed, and we loved her. Our nurseries were the two top rooms in the Headmaster's house. When I went away to school, 'Penny' stayed on to help my mother.

It seems to me now how extraordinarily free we children were in those 'safe' days; we could go along the Whitstable Road to Blean to buy sweets, or we could cross the road and visit the Oast House to sit among the drying hops, or we could spend a whole day in Church Woods, knowing where to find lilies of the valley, and there was no danger for two small children. How the world has changed! *Kidnapped* was only an eagerly read story by Robert Louis Stevenson.

I must apologise for straying into personal memories, but I was, after all, 78 yesterday, so I may perhaps be allowed just a little rope. But I can also recall several of the boy's names: Chris Grey, a farmer's son from Warwickshire; a very little boy, called Cheffins, who was allowed to play with me; a Chinese boy whose name I never knew, nor how he came there – the Methodist Mission, perhaps? – and two Kilner brothers, whose father gave us a beautiful green glass door-stop, which I, alas, broke a few years ago.

So goodbye K.C.! and thank you for starting me off so happily on this long journey.

Memories of the late J.C. Hosking (K.C. 1899-1905)

Written shortly before his death in 1981

I can't say I enjoyed my first year or two at K.C. because my mother died shortly after I got there and I had no one to come and see me, as most other boys did, at Prize-Giving days when parents were invited. Another reason was the presence then of a bully rejoicing in the nickname of Boxer. His joy was to collect a few of us, younger than himself, and what he called 'lion-time' us behind the gymnasium. One of the Lyles and I were frequent victims until we decided to end the persecution by going for Boxer together. We all three ended up with a little spilt blood and Boxer with a black eye. Miss Hicks attended to the repairs and, oddly enough, no one was punished. I suppose the masters had a pretty good idea of what had been going on and felt rough justice had been done. Anyway, that ended the lion taming.

One boy returned from the Christmas vacation with what one or two of us thought an excellent idea for making some extra pocket money. He had conceived it when he learnt what his father had paid for the mole-skin coat his Mother wore. The farms around K.C. were infested with moles so why not get permission from the owners to catch them? The farmers were delighted and lent us their traps. All we needed then was a skinning outfit, and four of us clubbed together and bought that from Gamages. The smell of the drying skins killed that enterprise!

After leaving K.C. I went to University College School which was then in Gower Street and it took me a long time to settle down there – the atmosphere being so completely different. For instance, returning from a cricket match against Mill Hill a boy about my own age confessed that he'd pawned his best suit to obtain the money to back a horse running the next day in the Derby. It lost, and when, later, I asked him how he was going to explain a missing suit to his mother, he replied that he had already acquired another, just like it, from Harrod's and charged it to his father's account there – no bother at all, because the family bought everything from that store and the item would never be noticed!

Memories of Percy Goble (K.C. 1902-6)

Mr. Goble lives in Worthing, and I telephoned him on his ninety-third birthday in 1983. In the course of a long and lively conversation I found his memories of his schooldays vivid and amusing.

Mr. Goble came from a Folkestone family, and boarded at K.C. He remembers that the rising bell was rung each morning at 7 a.m. by Mr. Webber, caretaker-handyman, who was one of the pillars of the school, as was his wife. The school was not then on mains water. Water came from two springs, one now underneath the main boiler room, and the other under the present Lower School. (It was this latter spring which caused Mr. Fisk, foreman builder in charge of building half of Lower School, so much trouuble in the 'thirties, as his memoir [see p. 72] shows.)

Mr. Goble spoke repeatedly about the quality and quantity of the school food, which he remembered as being poor. (It was not he, however, but his contemporary the late Cyril Bryant [K.C. 1905-1910] who wrote of a pudding called 'Mrs. Facer's leg'.) Once, he recalled, the tea tasted particularly foul and the boys complained to the master on duty. The source was traced to bars of yellow soap, dropped in the tea by the maids who were in the midst of a running feud with the boys. The boys lived on the contents of their tuck boxes and on snacks or sweets sold at the school tuckshop. He remembered the staff with respect, tinged with pity. They seemed to him in retrospect a down-at-heel, shabby, Dickensian lot, for the most part under-qualified. But they made up for their lack of qualifications by their undoubted skill in the classroom. They were mainly bachelors, and resident.

Mr. Goble retained two more vivid memories. The first was of the boys marching four abreast on a Sunday morning to St. Peter's Methodist Church. As they crossed the level crossing, local lads loved to threaten them and the cry would go up from the leaders of the K.C. troops, as they swung their mortar boards: 'Ware blags' (blackguards). The second was of the school's most solemn oath – 'I swear by the rats of K.C.' Mr. Goble insisted that rats abounded, and that a friend of his had trodden on one.

CHAPTER SIX

K.C. in
Alfred Brownscombe's
time (1911-34)

The Brownscombes took over the management of Kent College, suitably enough in view of Alfred Brownscombe's passion for sport, in the summer term of 1911. The change of headmasters made a striking impression. After Frank Facer's withdrawn dignity, there appeared a jolly, well-built, fresh-faced man aged 34. He seemed like a kindly farmer of middling prosperity.

Brownscombe had already been Head for eight years of a private school in Maidstone, Brunswick House, which he had attended as a pupil. He was a graduate of St. John's College, Cambridge, had taught at Truro School for a couple of years and captained Maidstone Cricket Club. I can find no record of his starting salary, but in 1923 it is recorded as £820 a year with board and lodging valued at £350. The salary was more than double that received at the time by his Second Master, John Hargreaves. Mrs. Brownscombe was to take an intimate part in the school's affairs, as Matron in charge of the boys' health and housekeeper responsible for their food. She was to be remembered warmly for the care she took of her charges and for the particular nursing responsibilities she bore during the period, not only of the war, but also of the immediate post-war with its terrible 'flu epidemic.

Under the new Head life continued much as usual, though the turnover of teachers must have been worrying, even in those days of lowly paid nomadic staff. Of the seven staff whom Brownscombe inherited, five had left within three years. Elgar, the drawing master, resigned at the beginning of the war. Only John Hargreaves remained. N.C. White became the first K.C. boy to win an Oxbridge award when he gained an exhibition at Trinity College, Cambridge. The summer picnics continued. Brownscombe turned out regularly for the cricket XI. The Old Boys expressed themselves delighted with the Brownscombes' hospitality on the occasion of the Whitsun cricket match.

Frank Facer had started a log-book which Brownscombe maintained. Occasionally he would make detailed entries recording the incursion of the outside world, such as that for 3 October, 1913: 'an airship, which was flying very low, went over our playing fields. Splendid spectacle.' Sport was well recorded in the log-book and the unbeaten record of the 1912 football team proudly noted.

The age distribution of the boys, together with their length of stay, continued much the same. Of the first 50 boys admitted by Brownscombe:

> 1 boy was aged 9
> 3 boys were aged 10
> 7 boys were aged 11
> 7 boys were aged 12
> 12 boys were aged 13
> 11 boys were aged 14
> 5 boys were aged 15
> 3 boys were aged 16
> 1 boy was aged 18
> <u>50</u>

Of these 50 boys:

> 8 spent 1 year or less
> 14 spent 1-2 years
> 12 spent 2-3 years
> 9 spent 3-4 years
> 3 spent 4-5 years
> 4 spent over 5 years
> <u>50</u>

Thirty-eight came from London and the Home Counties, four from the rest of the United Kingdom, and eight from abroad, of whom four were from St. Petersburg. There were no sons of clergy.

Sickness plays a large part in the log-book. The Easter and summer terms of 1913, for instance, must have been traumatic times for Mrs. Brownscombe and the Sanatorium staff. 'The amount of sickness which we had in March 1913 was unprecedented.' Twenty boys were in bed with influenza for a week or longer, and went to the sea for a few days to recuperate. No sooner had the boys returned for the summer term than one went down with measles and another with rheumatic fever. Soon 27 caught measles, and all inter-school cricket matches were cancelled, along with Prize Day. Numbers of entrants, however, rose steadily and by the outbreak of the First World War there were nearly 100 boarders, with six day-boys.

The outside world troubled the pages of the *Rampant* somewhat more frequently than it did those of Brownscombe's log-book, but not very much more so. The Easter term of 1912 saw the usual spell of sliding on iced ponds and tobogganing down 'Harbledown Hill', which I take to be the modern Duke's Meadows. It also coincided with a coal strike. Supplies at school held out, and the pessimists who feared that they wouldn't be able to return home for the holidays as the trains wouldn't be stocked with coal were proved wrong.

The July 1914 edition makes eerie reading, in the circumstances. In its pages not the least reference to the impending war is to be found. In this it strikes the same note of unruffled calm and contentment as Brownscombe's log-book entry for the summer term, 1914.

> Owing to a long spell of hot weather boys patronised the swimming baths freely.
>
> The annual picnic took place on 29 July, 1914. Herne Bay was visited and all enjoyed an excellent day's outing though the weather was too boisterous to permit the additional enjoyment of boating.

The security of his life and the happiness of his lot particularly impressed the editor of the *Rampant* that term who was moved to write:

> As we write the deep tones from the Cathedral tower reach us: the silence of the late evening is peaceably broken, and we are reminded that the end of term is close upon us . . . . We have, indeed, many matters for mutual congratulation: the term has been ideal; and the occasional diversions such as Old Boys' Day have greatly added to the pleasure of all. The cricket too has been very successful, and Harker is to be congratulated on having captained one of the finest elevens the school has ever produced . . . .

Term ended on 31 July. Great Britain entered the First World War on 4 August. In it, Harker was to be killed along with 50 other sons of K.C.

1914-18

From now on for the next four years the outside world of war hammered on the heavy doors of K.C. and shouted up at its dormitory windows. The inmates made no attempt to deny its demands, and one by one slipped quietly away. Brownscombe records the process in his log-book for the Christmas term 1914:

Mr. J.A. Ward B.A. who had only been with us one term enlisted during the vacation in the Royal Horse Artillery. Mr. Groom who was to have filled the place of Mr. Norman was gazetted a Lieutenant, in the East Yorkshire Regiment . . . . An Old Boys' Honours Roll was soon placed in the School Room and additions were made weekly. Linfield the senior boy enlisted in the Sussex Regiment . . . . On the day of the King's visit to Canterbury to inspect the Surrey Brigade before their de >artment for Egypt . . . Mr. Oldacre left and enlisted in the East Kent Mounted Rifles. His place was difficult to fill with the exams so near and the work was shared by all . . . .

The *Rampant* of December 1914 contained an article by an Old Boy who had just enlisted and was describing his army training. He used the *nom de plume* Novus Miles and called his article 'The New School'. The ethos and imagery was of the kind which later serving men were bitterly to deride, as the illusion of a war game turned into the reality of swamped trenches and comrades hanging on the old barbed wire.

We shall, I hope, at some future date celebrate an Old Boys' Day of this new school, and compare notes on the different classes. Nothing could be more cheerful than the spirit of the new armies. The difference is only a matter of years and a rather more serious end. But we lose nothing by taking into war the sporting spirit of our playing fields, and it is pleasant to think that so many K.C. Old Boys who 'played the game' in those fields under the K.C. flag are now, in the same spirit, playing a greater game under a mightier flag in the same old way, and are to be found in their places helping their side to victories greater than any in the past.

The *Rampant* of April 1915 contained a letter written by Maurice Gamon from the front line. Captain Gamon was to be killed in July 1916. He had been a secretary of the Old Boys' Club, a keen scoutmaster and a Sunday School teacher. Facer in his obituary (magazine of December 1916) called him our 'dear friend'.

I am writing in a little Belgian cottage kitchen, beside a curious bottle-shaped stove. The kettle is on the hob. I have just had a bowl of Oxo made from cubes sent to me by my dear little grey wolf cub, Deakin . . . . My pack stands on a corner table. My Bible, *Pickwick Papers, Punch, Land and Water* lie around. My servant dozes by the fire, and my scout orderly – not a boy scout, sad to say – sits patiently awaiting my orders, and I – I am writing at a nice round table by the light of a Catholic Church candle, which burns slowly and makes no grease.

Outside the wind is howling – the rain splashes against the window panes. It is cold and dark and miserable. Yet out there stand my faithful sentries, keeping watch – for we are only a few village houses away from the enemy; they hold half the village, and we hold the other. We meet in the middle,

41

where both sides have established themselves in houses with sandbags and furniture barricades and loopholes. Here I hope to stay four days . . . . Overhead small, splintered holes are left in the wooden 'ceiling' where shrapnel bullets have burst through. Outside is a scene of desolation – ruined cottages , tumbling walls, gaping roofs and broken furniture . . . .

Today ten men have been wounded upstairs. Others may be hit tomorrow as the tide of battle rolls on. Yesterday the good folk living here little dreamed of war; today the fight is going on; tomorrow children's children will tell how the English stemmed the tide of invasion, and held the last little bit of Belgian soil, together with the French and Belgian armies. And maybe the ruins of this, my little cottage, will be pointed out as the scene of one small incident in the far flung battleline . . . .

In my wildest dreams of boyhood did I ever imagine that I would one day command a blockhouse fort, barricading within 40 yards of the enemy lines? What a thrilling experience! Yet it all seems quite ordinary. Really, one goes about quite unconcerned, and only the occasional sight of a poor wounded fellow recalls one to the horror of it all, and the reality of war. It may be one's own turn next, but we refuse to think of that. Instead, thoughts turn to faces one loves at home . . . . Hey-day! What a row the Huns are making! I really must saunter round to see what the trouble is, and visit my sentries once again. And then to bed. Goodbye.

with love from
MAURICE GAMON

In the same magazine number the death is recorded of the first Old Boy, Sapper Sidney Pocock (1904-9), together with a letter written by a fellow Sapper to his father:

It is with feelings of regret that I have to inform you that your son, Sidney, was killed in action on 21 February, at about 3 a.m., and was buried on the field, and a wooden cross placed over his grave . . . .

There is one thing I should like to mention, as I know it will be of some consolation to you; it is that he died a Christian, and a more thorough one I have not yet come across for a fellow of his age. One thing myself and his other particular friends noticed was, we have never heard him use bad language in any shape or form, which was wonderful, considering the temptations that surround us in this life.

I have this day packed his effects in a box and am forwarding same tomorrow, but expect it will take a long while to reach you.

Always remember, sir, that he died the finest death in the world, serving his God, his King, and his country. Sappers Jasper, Lewis, Grandfield and Jones add their condolences to mine in this your very great loss.

I am, sir, his friend,
HUGH SANDAVER
(Sapper)

School numbers stood up remarkably well during the war. In

September 1914 there were 96 boys at K.C., of whom five were day-boys. In September 1918 there were 102 boys, of whom ten were day-boys. The age of entry remained much the same, though more were entering at 15, as this table of the first 50 boys who entered the school after the outbreak of the First World War shows:

2 boys were aged 8
1 boy was aged 9
2 boys were aged 10
5 boys were aged 11
5 boys were aged 12
11 boys were aged 13
9 boys were aged 14
12 boys were aged 15
3 boys were aged 16
50

They are spending slightly more time at K.C., compared to immediately pre-war days. Of these 50 boys:

7 spent 1 year or less
11 spent 1-2 years
13 spent 2-3 years
9 spent 3-4 years
6 spent 4-5 years
4 spent more than 5 years
50

Forty-two came from London and the home counties, two from the rest of the United Kingdom, and six from overseas. There was one son of a clergyman.

The great change that came over school life was the arrival of women teachers. The first to arrive was Mrs. Jackson, wife of a former French teacher, who had enlisted. She joined the staff in the Easter term of 1916. Miss Phare joined the following term and it was she who founded the Kent College boy scout troop, which was, from that time onwards up to the present day, to play such a large part in K.C. life. Miss Hargreaves, John's sister, taught for a year before her appointment as Headmistress of K.C., Folkestone. At one time John Hargreaves and the Head were the only male members of staff. P. Wardle Richards joined the staff in the Christmas term of 1917 and stayed until his retirement in 1955. He was to exert as great an influence on the life of the school during those years, as did Hargreaves during his years of service.

43

A cadet corps was formed in the summer term of 1915 and a rifle range built in the covered shed. Brownscombe became its Commanding Officer, with the rank of captain, while Lieutenant Hargreaves was his second-in-command. Its activities fill many pages of the Magazine while the 'red letter' days of its year – its fortnightly camp at Marlborough College – were looked forward to with great excitement. Old Boys' reunions and Prize Days were cancelled for the duration. In the number for Christmas 1917, 16 out of the Magazine's 41 pages were concerned with war news. One edition alone contained 19 names of Old Canterburians who had died in the last months, a surprising number of them, considering the social system of the time, non-commissioned. (Of the 51 old boys killed in the war at least one-third were non-commissioned.) Sport continued much as before though many of the football and cricket matches were now against army sides. Walter Price, the caretaker on whom K.C. was to rely, along with Jack Wallis, for 50 years from the time he joined Facer's school in 1900, won the Military Medal. Ration books were not introduced until the summer term of 1918. In that summer, two air-raids occurred on successive nights. One German 'plane was seen to be in flames. 'The gunfire of our own guns sounded rather disturbing,' wrote Mr. Brownscombe, 'fortunately no bombs were dropped; the only damage was that caused by our own shrapnel.' And though the Armistice, when at last it came in November 1918, was celebrated with fireworks and a sing-song, according to the Magazine's editor, it passed unnoticed in Brownscombe's log-book. He, poor man, was probably busy carrying trays for his wife while she nursed the 87 boarders out of 92 who succumbed to the famous post-war 'flu epidemic. 'Fortunately,' wrote the Head, and you can almost hear his sigh of relief, 'there was not a single case which gave rise to anxiety and by the end of term all seemed to have got back their health.'

1919-26

K.C. seems to have shaken off the war-time world very quickly. At the beginning of the summer term 1919 the numbers had risen to 121, 110 of whom were boarders. The Head announced in the log-book with justifiable pride that these numbers 'easily constitute a record'. The staff reverted to their all-male, largely bachelor pattern, with only a tiny nucleus remaining for any length of time. The Inspectors reported that staff salaries improved after the school came under the Methodist Board of Management in 1920. Some idea of their levels can be gained by the salaries of the two stalwarts of the Brownscombe years, Hargreaves and Richards. Hargreaves started in 1903 at £60 p.a. with board and lodging. In 1920 he was on £160 p.a. with board and lodging calculated at £70 p.a.

By the year of his retirement in 1936 his salary was £450 p.a. Richards started at £80 p.a. in 1918, with board and lodging valued at £70. He married at the end of the 'twenties, and reached £420 in 1931. He suffered a cut in salary, along with other teachers at the height of the depression, and by 1934 he was being paid £350 a year. It was said that the awe-inspiring Dr. H.B. Workman, Secretary of the London Education Department of Methodist Schools, which took over K.C. in 1920, liked to keep staff young and thus expenditure on salaries low.

Miss Phare left for a post in China in 1921, and was much praised for her work as Scoutmaster. She left behind her a flourishing pack of scouts, which John Hargreaves took over. The school, which was fully inspected by the Board of Education in 1919, seemed to be more securely founded than ever before, though it remained open to virtually any literate boy whose parents could pay the fees, between the ages of seven and 18.

The *Rampant* describes a life which seems very similar to that lived by the K.C. community before the First World War. The new editor, P.W. Richards, writing in April 1922, referred to 'the almost innumerable meetings of our several societies claiming almost every evening of every week'. There are accounts of the Natural History and Field Club, the Chess and Draughts Club, the Choral Society, the Literary and Debating Society, the Scouts, and the Cadet Corps, which continued under the command of Captain Brownscombe until its death in 1925. That Easter term of 1925 it was reviewed by Field Marshal Earl Haig.

Sport was revived with equal enthusiasm. In the summer of 1920 the cricket XI, which still fielded masters from the Headmaster downwards in its club fixtures, played 25 matches – a staggering number – and won 16 of them, losing only one. In the same year the hockey XI started up again. It also fielded masters alongside the boys and won all its matches, of which only one was against a school. R.T. Norman and D.K. Daniels won Oxford Hockey blues in the 'twenties. The life still strikes a *voyeur* from a later vantage point in time as strangely insulated in spirit. School was all-consuming in its interest and appeal to both boys and masters, the great majority of whom were resident bachelors.

When K.C. was transferred to the control of the Board of Management in the summer of 1920, the interest of the shareholders was eliminated, and the Board of Education, which had inspected the school the previous year, placed the school on its approved list. As well as Governors appointed by the Board of Management, the County Council appointed six Governors and one Governor was appointed by Canterbury Council. Grants were paid by the Board of Education, on condition that the school admitted a certain amount of scholarship boys each year. By 1925 the day pupils numbered 50, compared to the 14 of 1920. Boarding numbers remained the same at 120.

A science master, S.W. Rollings, had at last been recruited in 1921, and he spent part of his first vacation re-equipping the laboratories. He was succeeded three years later by Mr. R.A. Day, who stayed until the 'sixties, and became Acting Head for a term in 1959. Mains water reached K.C. in the summer of 1920. Electric light was installed in 1923. Altogether, the Inspectors in 1926 found the school considerably more efficient since it had been taken over by the Wesleyan Board of Management, though they said that intellectually K.C. did not yet compare with similar schools receiving grants from the Board of Education. This was hardly surprising since in that year there were only eight boys in the Sixth Form. Out of 37 leavers in the summer term of 1925, 30 were under 17.

1926-34

The 1926 inspection had given Brownscombe and his Governors renewed confidence. On Speech Day the head announced a new building scheme – a lecture room, two more laboratories and an art room would be built. Three years later a swimming bath was at last opened. In 1928, the Water Company built what was reputed then to be the largest water tower in England, and so provided K.C. pupils with a landmark which they could see on their return to school long before the buildings themselves, and the bath soon followed. No other single improvement ever gave the school so much pleasure.

The day-boy element steadily increased and topped 100 in 1930. By that time the decline in boarding numbers had begun. The old School Certificate – modern 'O' Levels – remained the highest ambition for most K.C. boys.

Only at one point, May 1926, the month of the General Strike, does the outside world reach the pages of the *Rampant*. The editorial struck a triumphant even a complacent note:

> Apart from the noteworthy fact that all members of staff showed themselves lovers of peace and order not unmixed with romance, with perhaps a taste for adventure in addition, by entering His Majesty's Police Force as Special Constables, the Great Strike had no effect on the inner workings of K.C.: another important illustration of the futility of direct action!

One is left wondering why no one at K.C. boarded a train at Canterbury East and alighted at Aylesham, three stops and five miles away. Here they would have entered a very different world. You have to look up the pages of the Dover local newspapers to realise that the miners' families were only surviving by courtesy of local charities, who provided them with soup-kitchens until the next year. Considering how well aware the K.C. boy had been during the first World War of the suffering of the front-line soldiers, it seems strange that nobody tried to enlighten him about the nature of industrial war.

Sport reached a peak of achievement during the years 1926 to 1930. In 1926 the cricket XI was unbeaten. Pat Vaulkhard, who was later to captain Derbyshire and on one occasion made 264 for the county against Notinghamshire, was a member of that eleven. H.G. Hubble hit 115 not out in one match, and finished with a batting average of 59.8. Two years later C.K. Herbert became the first K.C. batsman to complete 1000 runs in a season, a feat which would be unimaginable in today's abbreviated cricket season. In 1934 a youngster called Godfrey Evans scored two particularly attractive centuries for the Junior XI. They earned him a bat autographed by Jack Hobbs and donated by *The Star*. The school, under Hargreaves' direction, achieved a high reputation for its hockey. Tulse Hill's XI was at one time largely composed of old K.C. boys, and the club recognised this fact by sending a team down regularly in the Easter term. The club also invited Hargreaves in 1929 as guest of the evening at their annual dinner. The year before five O.C.s played in the Southern Counties' Trial. In 1933 *Hockey World* published an article on K.C. hockey, paying tribute to Joe Hargreaves' work and detailing the achievements of the school eleven and of its Old Boys.

In the world of alternative sport it seems that K.C. boys had taken to racing the local pigs, on Sunday afternoons:

> The pigs were commissioned in the manner of race horses entered for the Grand National. Dressed in their Sunday best – Eton collars, little black jackets, striped trousers – the rough and youthful riders, each seated precariously on his grunting steed, with nothing to steer by except the tail of the resentful porker, were about to negotiate the Tattenham Corner of the course when, as from nowhere, the arm of the law in the form of the Blean bobby appeared dramatically from among the spectators.

Before the general inspection of 1934, however, signs of trouble were mounting. Day-boy numbers held up well and stood at 119 in 1934, but the all-important boarding numbers fell catastrophically. In 1933 they were down to 83. In 1934 they reached 59. It is true, of course, that from 1929 onwards the country had been passing through the period of the Great Slump, though by 1934 the worst was over. But the slump alone cannot explain such a drop. It seems possible that, as with Frank Facer, Alfred Brownscombe stayed on too long, and that it might have been better if he had retired in the summer of 1932, when he and his wife had completed 21 years at the school. For the drop in boarding numbers was reversed by John Prickett, just as Brownscombe himself had reversed a similar slide in the last years of Frank Facer's headmastership.

Whatever the cause, the Inspectors referred to the financial loss incurred in the year 1933-4 and regarded the situation as serious. It was obvious to anyone who thought about the school's situation that considerably more boarders would have to be recruited, that boys should stay at K.C. longer and that a proper Sixth Form would have to be developed along with a better prefect system. (In 1934 there was one boy in the Sixth Form.) K.C. was, in fact, in no sense a public school, but rather a small, fee-paying grammar school whose pupils were gone by the age of 16.

In the summer of 1934 Alfred Brownscombe retired. The *Kentish Gazette* referred to his 'keen understanding of boys, his love of all manly sports and perennial cheerfulness.' The Mayor of Canterbury, Councillor Frank Hooker, merely repeated what so many wrote about Alfred Brownscombe when he said that K.C. boys learned to be happy from their Head, who radiated joy and gladness. Above all else 'the Governor' was attached to the Old Boys' Club. The most moving tributes paid to the Brownscombe family came from the club. The Old Boys wrote of Mrs. Brownscombe's 'willing helpfulness, tender sympathy and great kindness and sympathy' to them. One of the Brownscombes' daughters married a K.C. Old Boy, another a K.C. master, while their son became President of the Club. The Secretary, Cedric Bramwell, summed up their feelings:

> The Old Canterburian Club wishes to record . . . their very great appreciation of the kindness, goodness and splendid service rendered to them at all times, whether as Old Boys or as boys at school, by 'the Governor', his wife and family.

CHAPTER SEVEN

Memories of K.C. in Brownscombe's time

Memories of F.M. Adlam (K.C. 1910-13)

I joined K.C. at the half term of the summer term in 1910, which was I believe the first term of Mr. Brownscombe. I can well remember my first meeting with him in his study on my arrival. He was a well-built man and, when I knew him, a fit man and sportsman. He was also a disciplinarian, and I can remember one boy being thrashed by him in front of the school for thieving. I much enjoyed my stay at K.C. Mr. Hargreaves, the Second Master, was very keen on physical fitness. Mr. Brownscombe was well liked by the boys.

Memories of the late H.W. Skinner (K.C. 1910-17)

With the arrival of Mr. Brownscombe things changed. He was a much more cheerful type and would occasionally laugh. I have not much recollection of life until the 1914-18 War. We had sport every afternoon, cricket summer, football autumn and hockey spring, from 2-30 p.m. We were divided into four clubs according to age and size and had to play every afternoon, except Wednesday and Saturday when we had to watch home matches.

It was not very long after the War started, that the food started to deteriorate and we lost some of the younger masters. The Cadet Corps was organised (I found this very interesting), and took the place of sport for two afternoons each week. I enjoyed it. I found life more interesting as the War progressed, the food got worse, but three of us older boys were given more responsibility, taking prep. and some of the younger classes. It seemed to make us feel that we were helping.

Memories of the late A.L. Horrell (K.C. 1910-15)

I was too young at the time of the Facer/Brownscombe changeover to remember a great deal about it but, with hindsight, it appears that Mr. Facer was an introvert while Mr. Brownscombe was an extrovert.

Regarding the First World War, several masters disappeared and were replaced with inferior material, particularly as regards discipline. The Corps was founded attached to the Fourth Buffs. Mr. Brownscombe and Mr. Hargreaves were the two commissioned officers and I was a sergeant. Personally, the main fear was that the War would be over before I was old enough to leave school and join up. In the event, I left school and volunteered for the R.F.C. where I eventually became a commissioned pilot.

Memories of G.W.R. Brownscombe (K.C. 1915-24)

Son of Alfred Brownscombe

We lived in K.C. in a strange time – without realising how strange it was. Looking back it seems inconceivable that the school could have been carried on normally during those war years – carried on mostly by women. Domestic details naturally bulk large in my memory. The collection of ration cards for meat and butter and sugar at the beginning of term; the countless official requisitions and returns that were to be filled in; the 12-hour notice that all windows were to be covered at nights – no easy matter providing all the windows in K.C. with curtains. And I remember very clearly the excitement (though not the date) when the electric light was installed. When the batteries and engine were installed down in the cellar, for the first term the main switches were turned off during the day. I became a sort of unofficial switchman and most afternoons was sent for from the classroom to bestow again the miracle (in those days) of bright light.

My mother was acting as Matron from the time of Mrs. Jones' death in 1915 to September, 1921, as well as looking after all the domestic arrangements; all during the dreadful 'flu epidemic of the spring of 1919, when 91 out of 96 boarders caught it; 65 dinners taken up to the dormitories in one day – and with no outside nursing help at all! It says much for the health of K.C. that there was no single case of pneumonia.

At one time during the War, the male teaching staff was reduced to three – my father, Mr. Hargreaves and Mr. Richards. Lady teachers completed the staff, Miss Hargreaves, Miss Phare, Miss Fowler, Mrs. Jackson, Miss Lewis, Miss Harris – I often think how much more civilised we of that generation ought to be.

A service aeroplane crashed on the cricket field at K.C. one summer morning while the school was at breakfast. I think I was the only boy who saw the crash – saw the aeroplane swing on to its nose for a moment and then drop back at right angles to its track. Malicious rumour had it that the pilot had flown over K.C. the day before and been waved to by one of the mistresses taking a class out in the sun in the fields.

Talking of aeroplanes brings back thoughts of air-raids – the deafening din that six anti-aircraft guns made, all within a mile of K.C.; the Head's visits to the dormitories; his reassuring 'They've all gone over now; you can go to sleep'.

Memories of C.H.C. Suffolk (K.C. 1921-4)

The first thing to be said about K.C. in my day is that it was a happy place. There was an atmosphere of enthusiasm and cheerfulness about the school. A visitor to the school in 1920 would have found approximately 90 boys, practically every one a boarder, taught by a small staff in rather shabby surroundings. Five years later a very different picture would have presented itself. The number of boys had nearly doubled, improvements to the building had begun and the staff had increased enormously.

We were still lit by gas in 1920. An ingenious prefect used to rush round the school hall with a football bladder filled with gas, lighting the long rows of lamps that ran down the hall. On several occasions the lights quietly died out during prep. This entertaining phenomenon was caused by a youthful humorist who blew into one of the gas jets[9] in the corridor outside. The water supply, too, was subject to disconcerting vagaries. During the winter term of 1920, there was an aromatic flavour of carbolic about it due to the tank having been scoured out during the holidays. Quite frequently, owing to some curiosity of plumbing, the supply would fail altogether in certain dormitories, to the intense delight of the small fry[10]. All these things were soon to be altered, however. A new K.C. was to be created.

There was a notable absence of pettifogging rules and restrictions. In many schools it is the custom to present every newcomer with a list of the many trifling things which may not be done, but one does not recollect any such list of regulations at K.C. in my day. Discipline seemed to rely partly upon custom as established in the past and partly upon the rather unusual theory that boys have a sufficiently developed sense of the fitness of things to know what is likely to be considered out of order by the powers who may punish. Contrary to what may be supposed, this did not lead to pandemonium.

Memories of B.K. Chandler (K.C. 1924-6)

During the mid-twenties, the Canterbury and Whitstable Railway Line, running near K.C. with its half-mile tunnel, was a source of magnetic attraction to many pupils who drifted that way during the Thursday afternoon 'run'.

We would enter the tunnel with considerable excitement, stumbling over irregularly placed sleepers which had pools of dirty water between, but after barely 20 yards we were enveloped in Stygian darkness. We presumably had some knowledge of train times because it seemed a regular occurrence for a train to enter the southern end of the tunnel at about the time we had foolishly trespassed inside. We would look anxiously towards Canterbury and note the gradually diminishing 'halo' of light around the train. Suddenly, the 'halo' had gone and, with the tunnel rumbling, we would scamper out feeling that the engine would catch us at any moment. We would then hide ourselves behind nearby trees and bushes to await (for some five minutes) the emergence of the train travelling up the 1:56 gradient at about walking pace, accompanied by much smoke and steam. If we had placed halfpennies on the line, we would then collect our 'pennies'.

It would seem that no one ever considered that a train from Blean and Tyler Hill might be travelling down the gradient at 30 m.p.h. which would have put us in serious trouble.

Memories of J.B. Winter (K.C. 1923-30)

Lifelong supporter of the Old Canterburian Club and a Governor of the school for many years, serving as Chairman of the Finance Committee, and Chairman of the governing body

When I went to Kent College in May 1923 only the original building stood, with an ex-army hut from the First World War between the Whitstable Road and the playground. Included at the north end of the playground were two five courts and a row of lavatories. In those days no wash hand basins were provided.

It was quite a small school then with about 110-120 boarders, all housed in dormitories 1 to 6; dormitories 1 and 4 were inhabited by approximately 30 boys each and the other four had about 10 to 12 in each. Although we had a hot water system, the school was bitterly cold in the winter and spring terms; no water was available in the outside lavatories or in the dormitory taps in the coldest of weather. We were quite a tough bunch in those days and not expected to be particularly hygienic!

The ground and garden staff were comprised of 'Walter and Jack' – two stalwarts admired by the boys as they both played some cricket in the summer. The sporting activities were supervised by John Hargreaves, known as 'Joe' and, more lovingly, as 'Old Joe'. We had some excellent games players and achieved quite good results frequently against our rival schools in east Kent.

Meals were served in the dining-room with tables for 12 boys at each. Places were taken up at the beginning of each term. Each table had a prefect in charge and friends could sit together, but, having selected your table, you were required to sit at the same place for the whole of the term. The food was not very good in the early years but we did have waitress service; one maid to each table to carry the plates and dishes from and to the kitchen. Between courses, silence was the rule so that the staff would have no difficulty in clearing plates and dishes from the tables. The masters and matrons had a top table on the stage and this was graced at lunchtime by the Headmaster, his wife, and, when they were not at school, his daughters.

For the boarders, Sunday was a very long day. Twice in the day – except for the very young – boys went either to church or chapel. Blean Church meant a walk down the track past Keir's farm to the small Church set in the fields. Methodists and other Non-Conformists walked down St. Thomas's hill through the Westgate to the Methodist Chapel. In fact, the seniors did this twice every Sunday. We were not always blessed with very suitable clergy in either the Church or Chapel and most of us found Sunday rather a long and dull day as we also had to go out for a formal walk after lunch.

We had a very small number of boys who went on to university – not that there were a lot of university places then. A high percentage left school after sitting for Cambridge senior examinations and went out into the world to earn a living; this was not easy in the early 1930s.

The staff at K.C. were pretty mixed so far as ability was concerned, but there was a lot of character among them. Alfred Brownscombe was a jovial Headmaster – he had a kindly wife and three daughters at Simon Langton School with a son, Geoffrey, at Kent College.

John Hargreaves was a major plank in the school. He was not a great teacher or scholar, but much loved for his great interest in the sport of the school. He was very temperamental and got extremely cross nearly every half term and at the end of each term. We all felt that he hated losing us as he seemed to have no other interest in his life. During my years, several new masters came and were an improvement for our education. These included Roy Day and Sydney Spicer who taught physics and geography respectively. Throughout my time we had Dicky Richards to teach English through the school, MacGillivray for history, Tovey for chemistry. Ernie Baker taught the juniors for quite a spell and was loved by the younger boys, but we had the impression that he was not favoured 'high up'; I believe largely because he was not properly qualified, through serving in the First World War. E.H. Baker, who was on the staff from 1921-35, was at school until 1917. He held a London University diploma or certificate, which he took externally, and joined the staff at the age of 20. Matrons came and went as matrons and their assistants do. The domestic staff mostly changed frequently as domestic staff always seem to do. Each new term we boys watched anxiously to see who was new and whether there were any reasonable 'lookers' among them.

Kent College was a very friendly school in the 1920s; led happily by 'Governor' Brownscombe with a hard-working, friendly staff. Most of us made friends with other boys which have lasted all our lives. It was certainly a happy school in my era, despite being very cold at times. It produced quite a lot of characters and men of ability who have done well in various walks of life.

Memories of W.L. Blackshaw (1924-29)

Past President of the Old Canterburian Club, and one of its most loyal supporters

As I dip into the past, incidents from those now distant days flow into my head and reveal themselves with a vividness that is almost real; I think of night manoeuvres with the cadets, of trips to the Chatham Stream[11] and the haunted barn[12], of orange crush, of a certain prefect who took dormitory duty with a sword, of mumps and of Marche Militaire[13]; the competition between the East Kent and Cambrian bus companies, the craze for clique ties, fretwork and classroom fives. I recollect Basil Thornett's brilliant debating prowess, Henry Hubble's skill at the piano, and 'Piney' Hobson's success at melodrama. Twelve guinea suits[14], doughnuts[15], Mr. Spicer's signature, essays on Deans[16] and butterfly collars[17], should all claim a portion of this narrative for themselves.

The Old Virginian Club originated from the K.C. Fifth Form in 1928-9. Their classroom was a tiny room at the end of the old scout hut, and the piece of ground, now between the Chapel and the road, was known as Virginia Park. I think the majority of the staff looked upon the ten of us as a somewhat illiterate bunch, with more brawn than brains and little academic ambition. The late D. MacGillivray was our form master and coped with this most difficult crowd with considerable tact. Mac. was a brilliant man for whom we all had a very great respect, one that developed into an affection in later years. With Mr. Mac. as President, Mr. Spicer as

Vice-President and myself as Secretary, we formed the Club at K.C. and this continued to thrive for many years after we had left. We used to meet for supper in Canterbury, and had our own tie and club crest. The premature death of Mr. Mac. stunned us all, and was followed by the death of Ernest Cowper Field. Our meetings then became scarcer and finally petered out.

The 1928-9 period saw the organisation of playground games on a very satisfactory basis, and a comprehensive description of those titanic struggles can be found in 'Ambles Over the Asphalt' which is still in the possession of the author[18]. Football and hockey leagues were formed in their respective terms, and six teams – each being captained by a prefect – gave battle between 8.30 and 8.55 a.m. when the clemency of the weather permitted. The encounters were not only fast and furious, but provided great entertainment to the many spectators. The domestic staff displayed obvious enthusiasm, while even the masters occasionally indulged in a sly peep.

The late A. Brownscombe: Basil W. Burgess (K.C. 1922-28)

Committee member of the Old Canterburian Club, and one of its most loyal supporters

When I arrived with my mother at K.C. in September 1922, the 'Governor' greeted us both as though we were one of his family. The kindness he extended to a small boy of ten never altered throughout my school days and when I said 'good-bye' in December 1928 I knew then it would be impossible to meet anybody who would match his personality and thought for others.

Although the school may have lacked academic results, he instilled in us all honesty, sportmanship and true respect for others and one's country.

Kent College of My Time: Stanley John (K.C. 1924-8)

Past President of the Old Canterburian Club

At the age of 13 I had completed four years of study at a small French Ecole Primaire Elémentaire, the equivalent of which, I feel sure, could never exist in this country. My parents decided that the time had come for me to complete my education at an English boarding school, and I chose K.C.

I have always known that I had chosen the right school and at just the right time. That particular year, 1924, was to be a very special one in the history of the school. The chaos and disruption created by the First World War had given way to a more stable, normal way of life for most of us and the record intake of boys that term was largely made up of boys of a higher age group than normal. This ensured that the school was able to launch into a period of outstanding achievements, scholastically as well as sporting, which was to bring Kent College right up into the forefront of boys' schools in Kent and the South East.

The administration of the school was on very simple lines, being divided numerically into three houses, Blues under J.T. Hargreaves, White under P.W. Richards, and Reds under D. MacGillivray. They competed annually for the Facer Shield, a competition originated by the previous Headmaster in 1910.

As became a Methodist school, religion played a very big part in the our daily life due to the influence of the headmaster, his wife, and his family. We enjoyed daily hymns and prayers in the schoolroom during the week, and on Sundays we journeyed down to Canterbury to attend Chapel service, twice, on foot either way. We also welcomed the local Minister weekly at K.C. for talks in the library and supported enthusiastically all the bazaars and missionary efforts at St. Peter's Chapel. Where parents expressed a desire for some of us to be confirmed we were allowed to attend the Church of England services: in the mornings at Blean, and the evening at Saint Dunstan's in Canterbury. Confirmation in Canterbury Cathedral was an unforgettable experience for those of us who took part.

One of the main influences on K.C. at that time, and which I sincerely hope has remained until the present day, was the effect of the Old Boys and their association with the school. Their presence was always given pride of place by the Headmaster and staff and we were brought up to look up to what one might call today the 'end product' of the effect of K.C. education on boys of all kinds and from all parts.

Random Memories of K.C.: Michael Y. Horsfield (K.C. 1931-5)

Bentites

A form of punishment administered by prefects to boarders. The weapons varied from bedroom slippers to hockey sticks. Bentites were given to the last boy in bed in each dormitory. This did not encourage cleanliness in mouth or body. Bentites were also given in exchange for bad marks to enable boys to avoid being gated – three bad marks in a week meant gating. The sketch drawn by my father in one of his letters (*see Fig. 21*) illustrates the process.

Sundays

The last four Sundays of term were given specific names. I can't remember the order, but the names were as follows:

    Cough Sunday – boys coughed from time to time during the sermon;

    Yell Sunday – boys yelled during the last verse of the last hymn;

    Drop Penny Sunday – boys dropped their pennies from time to time in the service until they were received in the collection.

(There was an old-fashioned sweet shop at the bottom of St. Thomas' Hill, just before London Road, where many boys exchanged their penny for collection for two halfpennies. One was used to purchase licorice and other cheap sweets, and the other was a reduced offering to the Church or Chapel.) There was also Bash Hat Sunday – I can't remember the correct name for this one, but I think it was the last of the term, for boys bashed each other's straw hats until they ended up with nicks in the edges or the top hinged like a lid.

The gauntlet

The new pupils had to run down the corridors between the beds into the wash area and back again, while established boarders stood at the end of their beds armed with knotted towels ready to take a swipe at the new boys as they passed. The victims were expected to circulate until they dropped. Boys with beds in the middle row had two swipes at them.

The screen

New boys were expected to sit on the screen facing the beds and to sing a song while others swiped at them with knotted towels, the knots having been wetted for better effect.

Ducking

New boys were ducked in a full basin. The basins were very small but certainly seemed adequate from my experience as a new boy.

Ship wrecking

New boys were tipped out of bed in the early hours, mattresses and all, and their belongings were scattered far and wide.

The outside bogs

These were near to the fives courts at the end of the tarmac playground.

There was a common trough serving the cubicles. The seat was a plank with a hole it it. A trick was to float a tin lid with lighted candle down the trough to surprise a bare bottom.

Hymns for evening prayers

Boys were sometimes permitted to choose the hymn. Favourites were: 'Day is dying in the West', when R.A. Day was on duty; 'I met the good shepherd just now on the plain', when MacGillivray was on duty, for, as a Scot, his much used expression was 'just now'.

Mr. Fearon

There was a new French master named Fearon (I'm not sure of the spelling) who had his blooding in the hut. He was having a terrible time when he hit on the idea of mass caning. He marched us all up to a room in the school used for table tennis, formed a queue and systematically caned the lot of us. We all developed a great respect for him after that, especially when we learned that he was a swimmer of considerable repute. His nickname up to the time of the caning had been Pansy Fearon, but it fell into dis-use thereafter.

Cos Pond

St. Edmund's School opposite used to be called Cos (Clergy Orphan School) in my day. There was a pond on K.C. side of the road between the two schools which we called Cos Pond. There was great fun when this iced over, and when snow was on the ground snowball fights between the two schools took place.

Ma Maple's

A little shop near the school where we bought 'tuck' when running!

CHAPTER EIGHT

K.C. before the Second World War (1934-40)

K.C. entered the modern world when John Prickett became Headmaster at the age of 26. Until September 1934 the school still ran along Edwardian lines. Frank Facer would have recognised it as his school. With Prickett we enter the era of steadily expanding numbers, rebuilding, curriculum development, pupil-centred education and many other features of modern secondary schools. The K.C. of the 1980s is in direct and obvious line of descent from the school of the late 1930s. The Governors were looking for a young man of the greatest energy, drive and imagination to save the school. They found him in John Prickett. They backed him loyally and responded fully and quickly to his demands.

Prickett had been educated at Rydal and at Trinity Hall, Cambridge, where he had read Part 1 History and Part 1 Moral Sciences. After Cambridge, where he had taken a keen part in college sport, he had taught for a while at an Egyptian Government secondary school, before returning to Cambridge to take the Cambridge Certificate in Education. He then spent two years teaching French, history, and English at Quarry Bank High School, Liverpool, before being appointed Headmaster of K.C. on 11 July, 1934. He was married and his wife, who was French, played a very full part in the life of the school. They had no children. He arrived with a fully formed philosophy of life, and therefore of education, remarkable equipment for a young man in his mid-twenties. During the next 26 years he held consistently to the same liberal, Christian, humanist ideals.

He certainly moved fast. Within a year, the foundation stone of the new Junior House was laid. Joe Hargreaves, who ended his teaching career in 1936, took over the school's housemastership with the help of Miss Ashwell as Matron who, according to one of her small charges, 'reads to us every night when we go to bed, except on Saturday, when we listen to the wireless'. At his first Speech Day (1935) the new Head stressed the need to develop the school's numbers at the other end, by building up a decent second year Sixth, a process which soon began to get under way. A new block was built, which reflected Prickett's belief in the development of 'all-round' education. The block, which now stands by the Whitstable Road, contained a gymnasium, an art room, and a room for various handicrafts, including woodwork and metalwork. The dormitories were improved and the need for privacy recognised by the introduction of cubicles. The schoolroom became a panelled Assembly Hall-cum-Chapel, while the dining room was graced with curtains and its tables with napkins. The library was moved from the present staff common room to the old dormitory 3 on the first floor. The room was greatly improved by the use of the insurance money gained from the 1938 fire. A terraced garden was built under the inspiration of Mrs. Prickett on the school field side of the Junior School, and further gardens introduced between the new gym and crafts block and the Whitstable Road. The fields in front of the school, now the area of the tennis courts, Wesley House, and the First XV rugby pitch, previously used only by sheep, were levelled as football fields and tennis courts. Just before the outbreak of war, the old cricket pavilion was rebuilt and called the Hargreaves Pavilion, as a gift from the Old Boys. Only in the late 1970s has there been a similar building boom. Then, as in the 'thirties, members of the school community complained that they were never free from the presence and noise of builders.

All this activity was combined with the usual duties of a Head and with a fair amount of classroom teaching, particularly of the Sixth Form. On top of all this, John Prickett himself produced three school plays in the new Assembly Hall, *Abraham Lincoln, Saint Joan,* and *The Admirable Chrichton.* They were the first real school plays which K.C. had experienced.

The impact of the new Head's beliefs was equally positive. His ideas emerge from the pages of *Kent College Magazine* as clearly as they speak from his memoir (*see p. 64*). The full development of human personality; the importance of Christian education, both direct and indirect; the encouragement of self-education, as shown by his belief in the Dalton Plan; and of self-government within the school, as in his introduction of a School Council and his plans for elected prefects – all these were recurring themes with John Prickett. K.C. was offering careers advice and producing a Jazz band at a time when few other schools could claim such facilities, but John Prickett believed, with equal force, that it was fatal for a school to be isolated from the events of the outside world. At every Saturday Assembly he would speak about the affairs of the previous week. His belief in internationalism, his horror at the international arms trade, his outrage at the rise of Nazism and Fascism – all these were reflected in the life of the school. One wonders what his feelings were when the editor of the Magazine published an article in December 1935 by a German K.C. boy, H.W.G. Hefner (VA), which extolled the virtues of the Hitler Youth movement.

These ventures, when reviewed with the advantages of hindsight, can give a false impression of easy success. In fact, it is clear that two years after his appointment K.C. was close to closure, as the following episode, told to me recently by Mr. Prickett, illustrates. One morning in 1936 the Head looked out of his study window and saw the familiar figures of the Dean of Canterbury (the Reverend Hewlett Johnson, known to the Press as the Red Dean) and the Headmistress of the Simon Langton School for Girls walking up the school drive. When they were shown into the Head's study they said that they understood the school was for sale. The Dean was Chairman of the Langton's Governors and had accompanied his Headmistress, since the school was wanting to move out of Canterbury, to inspect K.C.'s site. The Head, ever courteous, though inwardly alarmed, showed them round. When they left he contacted his Governors, but heard no more about it. He suspects now that Dr. Workman, Secretary of the Methodist Education Committee, and a man accustomed to consult no one, had informed the County Education Officer that the school might be coming on the market in order to find out his reaction. Workman may well have been thinking: 'We might have to sell that school. Let's see whether we have a buyer.' Luckily, as Mr. Prickett's memoir records, the school's fortunes revived.

Two years later the school had 82 boarders. Then, just as the future looked promising, war came and with it, nine months later, evacuation. The revival of the school's fortunes, the Great Fire of April 1938, the coming of war in September 1939, and the evacuation in 1940 to Truro, are fully covered in Mr. Prickett's memoir. At the time of the Munich Pact, in September 1938, the school had arranged evacuation, in the event of war, to Queen's College, Taunton, but the arrangement had been cancelled. Dunkirk forced another decision, and one which would have to be taken and implemented at great speed. Let us leave Mr. Prickett to describe the move. As for the speed of the operation it is best illustrated by the Magazine. Its summary of the 1940 cricket season reads laconically:

Wed, 22 May	K.C. 161 for 4 wkts. Decl.
	Sir Roger Manwood's 35. WON by 126 runs
Sat, 15 June	Truro School 165 for 5 wkts. Decl.
	K.C. 86 for 6 wkts. DRAWN

CHAPTER NINE

Memories of K.C. before the Second World War

Extracts from the memories of H. Harman (K.C.1930-6)

H. Harman's full memoirs are to be found in the Jubilee Book.

I came to K.C. in the winter of 1930. To me it was all very novel and exciting. Beyond games and classes there was little provided to occupy our time, and I think from this condition was born the wealth of meaningless but intriguing customs that we looked forward to and maintained with vigour. In number and variety they were endless, and I think some are worth recalling, for nowadays they have almost disappeared, ousted by a fuller and more satisfying life.

One cannot forget the rituals of the last Sundays of every term. The first of these was dubbed 'Prig Pudding' Sunday, and on this day as the pudding was passed down the tables at lunch, all had the right to steal what they could as it passed. No joke, I assure you, if one was small and sat humbly below the salt. Still less a joke if the season was summer and the 'pudding' cherries or strawberries. Then followed 'Cock Hat and Show Rag' Sunday, when all and sundry wended their way to Church wearing their hats at extravagant angles and drooping eight inches or so of handkerchief from their breast pockets.

In the early 'thirties, to the rank and file of the school, the schoolroom was the centre of life. The library housed the upper ten of our community – the Sixth and the prefects – and for one half of the day it was open only to those exalted beings, jealously guarding their proprietary rights over armchairs and a fire. Here, teams were discussed and composed, prefects held meetings and wrongdoers were interviewed and castigated; but for us, the schoolroom was club, home and playroom. In this lofty room, dominated at one end by oak honours boards, the sunlight, stained by the colour-tinted windows, fell upon serried ranks of mutilated desks. Here we hatched our plots, read and pursued such hobbies as stamp and birds' egg collecting. I have seen bicycles brought in here and stood upside-down for oiling and repairs.

Life was a strange mixture of excitement and boredom. Probably the greatest hardship was the amount of time we had on our hands. Not all of us were made for games, and there was far too much vacant lounging. In summer terms it was easier. There were all the treasures of Blean Woods open to us, and we climbed trees, nested, explored, dammed up streams, or just wandered happily with our pockets filled with Mrs. Maple's bread and cheese. The masters really seemed to have little to do with us younger people. Doubtless they entered into the life of the school, and perhaps our elders, the Fifth and Sixth, knew them better than we did; but to us, knowledge of their personalities was restricted to classes with but few exceptions. Such authority as we came up against concerned the prefects, and their powers seemed limitless. Their rule was an uncertain volatile mixture of severity and carelessness – not altogether bad, by no means good. Now and again we suffered under a young sadist, but chiefly I remember healthy young sportsmen who troubled us little so long as we disturbed not their peace.

Between 1931 and 1934 the numbers of the school began to decrease. The result was, paradaoxically, a happy one. As a smaller community we became a more wieldy one, and a kind of intellectual revival set in. In 1931 the Literary and Debating Society was successfully revived. The following year saw the founding of the Historical and Scientific Societies. K.C., like the majority of young schools, has always had a scientific rather than an 'arts' bias, and the success of the Scientific Society was amazing.

In 1934, Mr. Brownscombe retired. With him left several of the staff and a great many of the elder boys. To us it seemed as though the end of the world had come, and we reassembled at the beginning of the Christmas Term with a great deal of excitement and speculation. I think most of us present will long remember Mr. Prickett's beginning-of-term address. We awaited it with mixed feelings – pleasure because we expected a harangue of the first order (dearly loved by all boys and other sentimentalists), resentment because we expected notice of new ways of doing things. But above all we were eaten up with curiosity concerning our new Headmaster. A new personality had come among us. I think if teachers ever completely realised how intensely critical their pupils are, they would be too terrified to open their mouths.

Mr. Prickett confounded all our reactionaries by a mixture of dignity and simplicity. In a few words he introduced himself to us, and then proceeded with evening prayers. There was no harangue, we were not bewildered by prophecies of a rooting up of all we were accustomed to. We were very mystified. It was all too easy . . . .

Once, two years later, during the solemnity of a Sunday evening service, as I pondered with satisfaction upon the newly created Hall, I saw again the air thick with the flying remnants of a Friday night 'bun fight', saw a bicycle upside-down in a pool of oil, and as a movement of the congregation brought me back to reality, somewhere high up in the honours board the unrepentant schoolroom winked a wicked eye.

Memories of John Prickett (Headmaster 1934-60)

I came to K.C. in 1934 during the worst recession Britain had known for many years. Unfortunately, the school was in no position to meet the impact of the recession. Owing to lack of capital its furnishings and equipment had been allowed to deteriorate to a very low level and the general morale was at a pretty low ebb. As a result, the number of boarders fell rapidly during the early 1930's until by 1934 it was as low as 55 and the Governors realised that unless drastic measures were quickly taken the very existence of the school would be called in question. This situation created a demand for a 'young and vigorous' headmaster who might have some chance in the long term of re-establishing the school on a sound basis. It was realised, at least in theory, that it would be a long haul.

So much needs to be said to explain how it came about that, at the age of 26, I was selected by a joint meeting of the Methodist Education Committee and the Kent College Governors, held at Westminster College (then in Horseferry Road), as the next Headmaster. No one could have been more surprised than myself, since in those days it was most unusual to appoint a headmaster under the age of 40 – and even that was considered very young for the job.

I was appointed in July 1934 as Headmaster of 'Harbledown School' as the Governors had decided to change the name, feeling, perhaps, that 'Kent College' sounded too grandiose for a school in such an impoverished state. On taking up my duties in September, however, I soon discovered strong feelings among many Old Boys and members of staff in favour of the original name and a far stronger sense of loyalty to the school and its traditions than I had been led to anticipate. One of my first recommendations to the Governors, therefore, was that they should revert to the original name for the school, which they agreed to do[19].

It was something of a shock to discover on arrival that my Second Master, Mr. J.T. Hargreaves, was 58 years old and had already been on the staff for 30 years. It should be recorded that he warmly welcomed the changes I began to make and gave me his full support in the battles which sometimes had to be fought to get them implemented. John Hargreaves

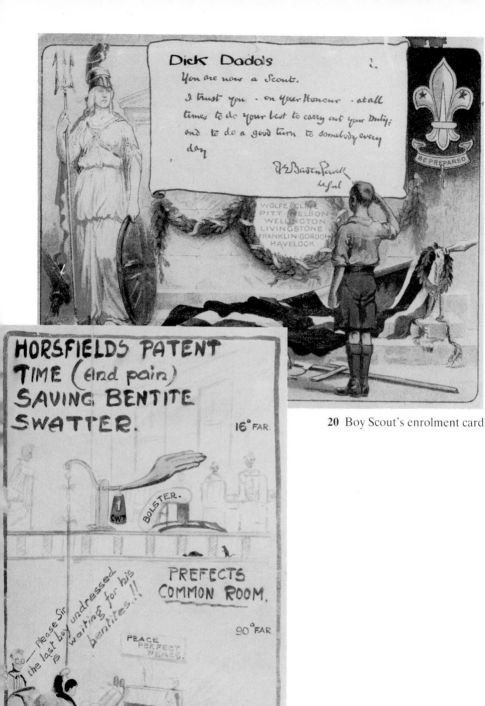

20 Boy Scout's enrolment card

21 Bentite swatter (*see Random Memories of K.C. by Michael Horsfield, p. 56*)

K.C. DURING THE 1920s

22 View from t[...]
when the Rough Common[...]
really crossed a rough co[...]

23 The Library, now
the staff common room

24 The Entrance Hall

25 The swimming bath – opened July 1929
– one of Brownscombe's ambitions achieved

26 The Large Domitory
with its *three* rows of beds

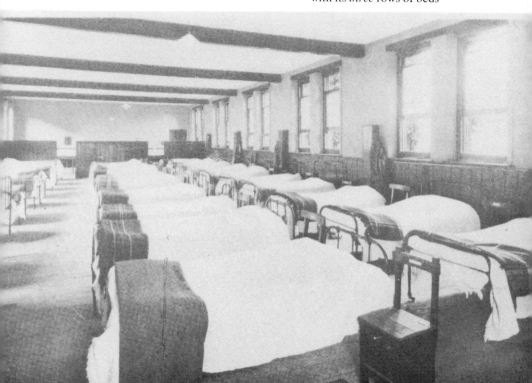

27 The new Headmaster,
John Prickett (Headmaster 1934-60)

28 The schoolroom becomes the new Hall
– one of John Prickett's first conversions

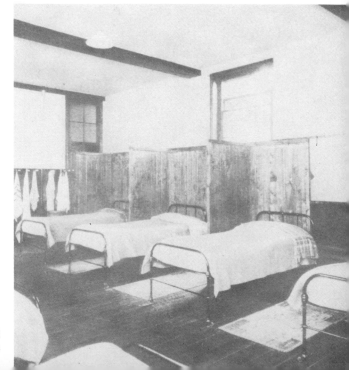

29 The beds are provided
with cubicles

30 The workshop block

31 Aerial view of the workshop block and the first phase of Junior School

32 Junior School completed

33 Some of its first inmates

34 Pets' Corner

35 A winter scene

36 and 37 The Great Fire

was a great character, to whom the school owes much for his dedicated service for more than 40 years.

My priorities of policy were to re-equip the boarding side, to appoint some well-qualified younger members of staff, and to extend the age limit at both ends by building up a Junior School and a good second year Sixth.

The Secretary of the Methodist Education Committee at that time was Dr. H.B. Workman, an eccentric genius whose works on mediaeval monasticism are still considered essential reading for historians dealing with that period. He was also Principal of Westminster College and a former President of the Methodist Conference. It would have shocked many Methodists of that era to know that shortly after my appointment he invited me to have lunch with him at the bar of a pub. in Strutton Ground, ordering half a pint of bitter for each of us.

Dr. Workman also had the reputation of being something of a financial genius. It is perhaps not surprising that with all these gifts he had a tendency to be autocratic, to act first and consult afterwards. This tendency led to some explosive situations both in his relationship with headmasters and with his own Education Committee.

For me, the crunch came in 1936. The Governors and the Methodist Education Committee had agreed to finance new buildings (the further half of the block, to be known temporarily as the Junior House, and the Workshop Block near the Whitstable Road) and had re-equipped the boarding side in the main school. But it takes some time for such improvements to have any effect on admissions. The money had been spent and there was little to be seen in return. Dr. Workman, therefore, conceived a plan, incredible in these days, for a 10 per cent cut in all staff salaries. There was also to be a bar on increments after the first five years. These proposed measures I fought with some tenacity and still have in my possession letters exchanged and reports written about them.

I was fortunate in having the support of a small group of dedicated Governors who were prepared to back me to the hilt and who went with me to London to put our case to the Education Committee. Two of them, Alderman Rose of Sandwich and Walter Seager, were Old Boys and I was deeply grateful for their support. The cuts were never made and the five-year bar on increments was abolished.

One significant 'change of use' at this time was the removal of desks from the schoolroom and the gift of 200 chairs by Old Boys to equip what now became the Hall, to be used for Assemblies, plays, concerts and school services.

By 1937 the scene was already beginning to change. Lord Northbourne had laid the foundation stone of the new buildings in 1935 and Lord Cornwallis opened them at Speech Day 1936. By 1937 the new Junior House was almost full, and for the first time for several years our income exceeded our expenditure. This brought a letter of congratulations from the Methodist Board of Management on 'the very much improved position in which the school stands financially' and a covering note from Arthur Atkinson, Clerk to the Governors, saying 'I never remember the school extracting such a testimonial from the Board of Management before!'

What of the academic side? I wrote an article for the *Kent College Magazine* shortly after my arrival questioning the fostering of the competitive spirit in school work through the mark system, form orders, and other similar devices, and asking whether effort could be equally stimulated by encouraging co-operation instead of competition, and joy in the creation of something good or beautiful for its own sake or for the sake of society as a whole. 'Many kinds of practical, creative work are being encouraged,' I wrote, 'and the tradition fostered by a purely classical education that manual work is degrading, or on a lower plane than mental work, is gradually being broken down.' With hindsight this may all appear somewhat naive and idealistic, but it was the kind of educational philosophy that lay behind the building of the workshop block with equipment for woodwork and metal-work, with a spacious art room on the first floor, and the introduction of individual work along the lines of what was then known as the Dalton Plan. Boys in certain forms were set an assignment for a fortnight and, during afternoon periods, they were free to choose on any particular day what work they would do. They would go to the subject room they selected where a specialist master would be present to offer advice to individuals when it was asked for, but not to teach a class in the conventional manner. Record cards showed the number of units of work completed in each subject at any particular time.

Another result of the attempts to give the boys more responsibility was the creation of a School Council. At first it was little more than a court to which grievances were brought and passed on to the staff. Later it was re-modelled and given more power. It was revived in a modified form while we were in Truro during the war. After the war it seems to have been lost without trace[20].

Already there was an increasing number of boys from abroad and especially from Paris. This may have been partly due to the fact that Mrs. Prickett was half French, and French parents were glad to find people who could talk to them in their own language.

In 1936 we welcomed the first of a series of German hockey teams and began our visits to German hockey festivals. These were greatly enjoyed and only added to our distress when international events rudely interrupted them.

In 1937 the field immediately in front of the school buildings, until then rough grazing for sheep, was tamed by a motor roller and a gang-mower and prepared for football in the autumn term. Four tennis courts were ready for the following summer.

School plays performed during these years included *Abraham Lincoln* by John Drinkwater (1935) with H. Harman in the name part, Bernard Shaw's *Saint Joan* (1936), with W.E. Mitchell playing Joan at the age of 13, *She Stoops to Conquer* (1937), *Macbeth* (1938), with Sidney Haynes as Macbeth and W.E. Mitchell as Lady Macbeth, and Shaw's *Androcles and the Lion* (1939) with Tony Carter as Androcles.

In 1937-8 we were trying to raise funds from the Methodist Education Committee for the completion of what was then known as the Junior School (now Lower School). We were told that Viscount Runciman, Treasurer of the M.E.C.[21], had refused to allow capital expenditure for this purpose. He was, however, persuaded to visit the school to make his own assessment of the situation and in January 1938 I received a letter from Dr. Workman saying, 'Viscount Runciman was very delighted with his visit to Canterbury on Friday last, and expressed himself to me in the highest terms of what he saw.' The result was the completion of the 'Junior House' in time for the opening of the new school year in September 1938.

In April 1938 came the Great Fire reported with dramatic headlines and photographs in the *Kentish Gazette* and the *Kent Herald*.

It was on Saturday, 2 April, while the school were playing the Maori Club (New Zealand Shipping Co. Ltd., London) at hockey, that flames were noticed coming from one of the dormitories. The game stopped and the players ran to form a bucket chain on the main staircase. I was in my study talking with prospective parents whom I had just shown round the school (parents of Tony Ware of Maidstone) when a boy rushed in to say the school was on fire. Five brigades eventually arrived and managed to limit the fire to the top floor (dormitory 6) and two masters' rooms, though other rooms on the first floor (dormitory 3 and other masters' rooms) were seriously damaged by water. The tower above the central stairway caught alight and crashed into the front drive. It was never replaced. The Headmaster of St. Edmund's School generously offered accommodation in his Sanatorium for the boys from the damaged dormitories. Telegrams were sent to all parents to say that no one was hurt and giving the time when their sons would arrive home on the following day[22].

Reconstruction began almost immediately and it provided the opportunity for considerable improvements in the damaged part of the buildings. Dormitory 3 and a master's room were replaced by a reference library, the poky little staircase which ran up to the subs. room and a small classroom was demolished and replaced by a changing room on the ground floor, and lavatory accommodation plus an additional master's room on each of the upper floors, with access from the main staircase.

After Mr. Chamberlain had promised us 'peace in our time' in 1938, only one year later came the outbreak of war. The following extract from the Editorial of the *Kent College Magazine* for December 1939 described some of the changes this entailed.

> Even before hostilities started, the staff and a daily increasing number of boys were in residence, busy in a seemingly endless attempt to cover the vast acreage of glass about the place . . . . The long hours spent in the atmosphere of imprisoned artificial light have fostered the growth of hobbies and reading.

'We had our own concrete underground air-raid shelter behind the Pavilion and beyond the swimming-bath. I expect a team of excavators could still locate it. It was rarely used . . . . On one occasion we spent part of the night underground, but it was very cold and damp and the following day one junior developed pneumonia. After that we were less eager to move as there appeared to be little danger of bombing in the Canterbury area at that time.

One interesting development during the autumn of 1939 was the arrival of the Pilgrim Players under the direction of E. Martin Browne (the collaborator with T.S. Eliot in the writing and production of his plays). He and his wife, Henzie, had stayed with us when producing Eliot's *Murder in the Cathedral* for the Canterbury Festival and both Eliot and Christopher Fry had stayed at K.C. during these festivals. Now his group of Pilgrim Players needed a headquarters where they could rehearse the plays, make costumes, properties etc. before they could set out on tour. A school, with all its facilities, was ideal for this purpose and when I invited Martin to make K.C. his headquarters he readily accepted. The first play they prepared was *Tobias and the Angel* and the first performance was given in the school Hall.

In the spring of 1940 the German breakthrough in Belgium with the threat to the Channel ports made the whole situation more precarious and I had to make plans for a possible evacuation of the school. On telephoning Dr. Magson, Headmaster of Truro School, I found that he had been anticipating such an approach from Kent College and he immediately said that he would co-operate in every way possible. I therefore went down to Truro and spent some time with Dr. Magson visiting a number of large country houses in the vicinity of Truro which might possibly be able to accommodate our boarders. On our visits we frequently met a group of army officers looking for places to requisition for the army. Eventually we went to a hotel known as Tremorvah, conveniently within walking distance of Truro School, standing in its own grounds, with a large dance hall which could be used as a dormitory, and a playing field. I asked the manager if he would be prepared to close down within a week and let the whole place to us for the duration of the war. He called a meeting of his Directors that same evening and by the following morning they had agreed to let it to us for a rent of £1000 p.a. for the duration.

I returned to Canterbury passing on my way through Kent trainloads of troops returning from Dunkirk. On my arrival I found a message from the Mayor asking to see me. He told me that he had just returned from the Ministry of War where he had been told to inform all schools and other educational institutions that if the Germans landed on the Kent coast no one would be allowed to move. (In Belgium the roads covered with refugees had hindered the movement of troops.) If, therefore, we wanted to move we must do so at once.

At that time Gorringes of London ran the school Tuck shop and through that connection I knew one of the Directors. I phoned him and asked if he could supply us with several large vans to remove all the school beds, desks etc. down to Truro. He agreed to provide some vans and Pickfords supplied the rest. All the boys resident in this country were then sent home with instructions to reassemble in Truro one week later, and largely through the superhuman efforts of Ray Lance, the Bursar, exactly one week later the school opened in Truro.

K.C. in the 'thirties: Barry Watson (K.C. 1934-8)

Past President of the Old Canterburian Club

My first visit to K.C. was on a hot Saturday in August 1934. I had travelled with my parents from Watford to investigate the possibility of my becoming a boarder in September. I have no recollection of the journey, or of Canterbury, but only of seeing John Prickett, the newly appointed young Headmaster, surrounded by beds and other school furniture, as we walked into the front drive. Even to me, just 13, the Headmaster looked young, but he immediately impressed me as a most courteous and kind man, who would obviously stand no nonsense.

I was accepted, and one evening in mid September joined a crowd of boys and parents at Cannon Street Station, waiting on the platform for the Canterbury train. My mother kissed me, the train chuffed out and carrying an attaché case with my initials on, wearing my K.C. boater, I was on my way! As a 'new bug' I was left rather alone and the other boys chatted about holidays, the new term, and the new Head, whom none of them had met. When I hesitatingly mentioned that I had met him, I became a centre of interest, and was naturally quizzed about the 'new man'. What little information I was able to give was, I gathered, somewhat suspect!

The prospect of sleeping in a dormitory with 30 other boys was somewhat daunting to a rather timid only child, but in fact I soon settled in and accepted the excitements of pillow fights, 'chariot racing' and 'running the gauntlet', which were normal before 'lights out'. I must have slept well, as I was roused by the sound of the hand bell – rung outside each dormitory by the Prefect on duty.

I was assigned to White House (later Godwin) with P.W. (Dickie) Richards as housemaster. He was to have a great influence on my personal and cultural development. His interest in books, natural history, and music were infectious, and I owe him a debt which I know many Old Canterburians share. He invited the new boys round to his house, 'The Fig Tree', in Rough Common, where, with his gracious wife, Enid, we were made to feel very much at home, with cakes and tea round a blazing open fire.

Members of staff, at first just names on a timetable, quickly became personalities, especially those who 'lived in' – Sydney Spicer (Spic) who with his beautifully produced maps, and epidiascope in a darkened classroom, became for me geography personified, as well as the person who on Wednesday and Saturday afternoons handed out sixpences from our allowance to spend in Rough Common or perhaps Canterbury. New members of staff were arriving by the mid-thirties and the trio Sidney Haynes, Jackie Crumpton, and Douglas White, all so different, and yet so characteristic of K.C. at this period, ensured that our lives, both within and outside the classroom, were never dull. Each in his own individual manner was a first-class teacher, and all three were fine sportsmen.

K.C. in the 'thirties: Derek Seager (K.C. 1932-9)

Past President of the Old Canterburian Club. His Father was at K.C. at the beginning of the century and contributed his memoirs to the Jubilee Book.

Sadly many of my contempories, in fact the vast majority of those names appearing on the organ shield as having lost their lives in the 1939-45 war, were my class mates, and it must be remembered that in the early 'thirties the total school only numbered about 100, of which the day-boys did not 'count'. There were also a number of farmers' sons living within a reasonable distance who were called 'weekly boarders', leaving the school on Friday night, or Saturday lunch time, till Sunday night, so the full time boarders occupied dormitories 1, 2, 4, 5, and 6. I cannot recall 3, though there should have been one.

Each dormitory had a sleeping-in Prefect, and at some stages a Sub-prefect, whose word was law, with the power (physical) of wielding the slipper. They appeared on my first night, at the age of ten, when the cry came out, 'Last three in bed'. The fact that all the old residents washed (screened) and undressed for bed in seconds flat, meant little to a 'new bug', and I felt not a little hurt in more ways than one to be invited to bend over my bed to receive three of the best 'bendtights'. I was rarely last in bed after that, but, although there were exceptions to the rule, most of the Prefects in the pre-Prickett era were too handy with a slipper and even offered to reduce conduct, or detention marks, at the rate of three belts to a mark.

Little reminiscences crowd the memory, often associated with particular members of staff. Many of my contemporaries from 1932-9 will recall Alfred Brownscombe's uncanny ability to flick a letter accurately at mail distribution up to the full length of the hall, his strong tenor voice at both Assembly and in the Choral Society run by Ernie Baker. He was the last master I can recall with pince-nez, who shared the maths department with Donald MacGillivray, a brilliant mathematician, whose death at a comparatively early age was mourned by the whole school, and whose funeral service was held in the school. Joe Hargreaves was a tyrannical but loveable Yorkshire man who smoked a nauseous mixture of St. Bruno's, and Three Nuns. As First Master he kept a fair but firm hold on the discipline. A keen sportsman and coach in all games, he also ran both weekly scout meetings and many of the more ambitious scout camps. I remember the uncanny accuracy of Spicer and, in his turn, Crumpton, with the chalk at a sleeping, or non-attending boy, and both men's stentorian voices calling, 'Come in' to us timorous beasties at the common room door. I recall P. Wardle Richard's nature walks through the Pine Woods, Bill 'Worsel' White [23], whose attempt to lay on a public thrashing in the school Hall was frustrated by the Prefects, and Nobby Fearon's blue for swimming.

I suppose no recollection would be complete without reference to two other stalwarts of the era: Roy Day, who was always bemoaning the loss of a pin, and who had the knack of making even physics interesting and Douglas White who brought (sadly not to me) the same kind of inspiration to maths, and a keen coaching flair to both tennis and his first love – hockey. I am privileged to have enjoyed his friendship.

The standards of food at the school received a fillip in the appointment of Joyce Miles who arrived at about the same time as John Prickett, and brought a more varied menu within the restrictions of her budget.

Mention must also be made of the ground and domestic staff. Walter

71

Price came as a boot boy, about the turn of the century, and was joined by Jack, from whom he was inseparable and who coped with everything from the pitches to the boiler. Nothing was too much trouble, and they laboured unstintingly on the school's behalf. Similarly, in the kitchen, I remember a family of three sisters, the senior being the Governor's maid. They wore the old-time maid's uniform, had to put up with a lot from both boys, and staff, and worked a long day.

The Building of Junior School

Mr. Fisk of 37 Rough Common Road, Canterbury, recalls his part in conversation with the Editor.

Mr. Fisk, who is now retired, is a Geordie who migrated south during the early 'thirties when work was desparately short. He decided to join his brother, who was working for a building firm in Tenterden, and at 24 was appointed Foreman Bricklayer for Clayson of Lyminge, who had contracted to build the first part of the Junior School building, which was started in 1935. The building was completed in about seven months.

One of the main problems they faced was the underwater spring which still lies today under the new building's boiler house. Mr. Fisk was unmarried at the time and had digs in Lovell Road. As he lived nearest to the site he was expected to walk across the games field before he went to bed each night to check that the pumps were working.

The laying of the foundation stone by Lord Northbourne on Speech Day 1935 was a Public Relations job. Mr. Fisk himself laid the actual stone some weeks later. He also laid another stone inside the cavity wall with the name of a boy from Wingham on it, which presumably still stands there. He had grown friendly with the boy during his months on the job.

He remembers that the Directors of the firm were Methodists, but it seems doubtful, from his memories, if all the men were of the same persuasion. Mr. Fisk remembers three of his colleagues in particular. There was the general foreman ('The General'), afflicted with stomach ulcers, who lived on Milk of Magnesia and had a permanent white streak running down from either side of his mouth to his chin. He collapsed on the job one pay day and died at an early age. There was the scaffolder, a likeable, cheerful man with a bad stutter, who was in the habit of waking up on Monday mornings, and going through his pockets. If he found two shillings or so there he wouldn't come in to work, but spent the day in the pub., where he wouldn't do so badly, with beer at tuppence a pint. The next day he would appear on the site as if nothing had happened, engage in an upper and downer with the General or the Governor, but would soon be working again.

But of all Mr. Fisk's old mates the one that stood out most vividly from the past was a Cockney hod-carrier. Very much a loner, he worked harder than any hod-carrier of Mr. Fisk's acquaintance, and won universal respect. He spent every minute working, spoke little, didn't smoke and never drank with the rest of the men. He appeared to save most carefully every penny that he earned. Then, at the beginning of one week, he failed to appear, and was gone for three weeks. He was assumed to be 'laid up' with illness, but one evening Mr. Fisk met him by the Beaney Institute, utterly and incapably drunk. Mr. Fisk, who had taken to the man, inquired of the hod-carrier's landlady, who thought the world of him, why he was absent so long. It appeared that he was in the middle of a long bender, a drinking spree which occurred with cyclical regularity, and which the man approached carefully and deliberately. He would regularly pay £5 in advance to his landlady to cover the next month's lodging charge and then proceed to set sail on his strange and solitary voyage. Mr. Fisk never saw him again and one takes it that a new hod-carrier was hired.

CHAPTER TEN

Exile in Truro (1940-5)

K.C. was to spend five years at Truro, and inevitably they were thought of as years of exile. To Dickie Richards, a Cornishman who had long waxed eloquent about the delights of his native county, the move must have appeared something of a bonus in his working life. To others on the staff it became increasingly a burden. Spicer's bitter letter to Mr. W.L. Blackshaw, which the latter kindly sent me and which is reproduced on p. 78, illustrates those feelings at their most despondent. (Spic was reported to have said that when he finally left Cornwall he would, before he crossed the Tamar Bridge, turn round and spit over the boundary.) But to others again, and to many boys, the move inaugurated a way of life which was more domestic, small-scale, and imaginative than the regimented life of a boarding school, however humanely administered.

About 80 boarders, the great majority, left Canterbury in June 1940. Sixty or so day-boys joined Simon Langton Grammar School for Boys, where they formed what were called 'sub-units' of K.C. Within three months the Langton, too, was to be evacuated to Wantage. From September 1940 onwards Truro and K.C. merged for academic purposes and for sport, though K.C. played fixtures against other schools and in Truro house competitions fielded K.C. sides. The Junior School remained separate. The Truro Headmaster said frankly that the academic arrangement saved his school. The departure of so many of his teaching staff for the forces would otherwise have presented him with insoluble staffing problems.

K.C. retained its own identity. At first, 30 senior boys slept in the Truro gym, under the control of Douglas White, before he left to join the R.A.F. The others lived in Tremorvah Hall, the hotel which K.C. took over, and which had its own wooded grounds. Most of the K.C. boys were sleeping there soon. Those who couldn't sleep there were accommodated in nearby houses, but to them, too, Tremorvah was home base. Here they spent their leisure, did their prep., and ate all their meals. David Spencer, Tremorvah's housemaster until Arthur Gibson succeeded him half way through the war, described house life in the *Kent College Magazine* in 1942:

I once heard Tremorvah described as 'K.C.'s Little Grey Home in the West'. To many of us the 'home' can never be anywhere but Kent. Nevertheless Tremorvah has the atmosphere of a home . . . .

There are the allotment plots where many boys of all ages may be seen each evening sticking peas or peering anxiously at tardy marrow growths; the hobbies room, which Mr. Hargreaves has fitted out at Tremorvah, and which keeps a good number of people occupied on wet days, and where many interesting things have been made, ranging from pipe racks to railway stations; and that other hobbies room, which, for some reason or other, is sometimes called Mr. Hargreaves' room – perhaps because he is allowed to sleep there – where it is always extremely difficult to locate him among the throng of occupants, mostly either billiard fanatics or card-sharpers; then there are the numerous outhouses that groups of boys have made their own and furnished according to taste; the evening cricket outside the staff room in the square in front of the hotel – so far, I believe, no one has broken a window. Then there were a few plays at Christmas time – an Elstow play produced by Bush, a pioneering effort which led to more; two one-act plays, and a staff pantomime, composed by Messrs. Spicer, Spencer, and Sullivan, but not apparently produced by anyone; and a Three Corners' play, *The Monkey's Paw*, at the end of the Easter term. *Journey's End* is in preparation for the end of the summer term. The bicycles swarm about the place like flies – that is, when they are not undergoing repairs which, to judge from the number of them forlornly upturned outside the garages, would seem to be their constant fate.

Three years later came V.E. Day, also recorded in the *Kent College Magazine*

On 8 May the whole school swarmed down the Malpas Road, those with bicycles acting as ferries to the younger boys, and soon a vast flotilla of rowing boats was racing for Roundwood. All arrived safely – though some were a little belated – and as the weather was perfect a grand time was had by all. In the evening a great bonfire was built, on which was burnt a most realistic effigy of Hitler, typifying his eternal punishment in the nether regions. There was community singing in which Mr. Macgregor took the lead on a piano dragged on to the terrace for the purpose. The evening ended fittingly with prayers around the glowing embers in thanks for a great victory and glorious day.

As during the First World War, the school Magazine, like the *Old Canterburian News-letter*, contained pages of news about O.C.s and ex members of staff fighting in the forces. Thirty-eight Old Boys were killed during the war. But there is none of the intense patriotism, often over-stepping into jingoism, which speaks from the pages of the First World War Magazine. Nor is there any of the earlier glorification of war. Rather there is a sad, realistic determination to win the war, and to face the consequent price of victory, simply because there is no alternative. One of the Head's Speech Day comments in 1942 strikes one as particularly perceptive. At a time when there was much euphoric talk of the reconstruction that must come after the war, and of the new society which victory would introduce, John Prickett warned his audience,

> We are getting used to this war . . . . We are getting used to the idea of killing and our sons are being brought up in an atmosphere of killing. Those who are crowned with glory are those who can kill most or invent some machine which is a more effective killer than any other in existence . . . . We believe war to be the lesser of two evils. It is nevertheless a great evil. And evil things have evil consequences. There is too much easy optimism about the sort of world we shall have after the war. Believe me, men do not gather grapes of thorns or figs of thistles.

The most obvious legacy which the school brought back from Cornwall was rugby football. Rugger had been introduced in the autumn of 1940 instead of hockey, and was played in both winter terms, along with football. Already the influential voice of Joe Hargreaves was being raised on behalf of the recognition of rugby as the school game of the autumn term to the exclusion of football. (No one seems ever to have suggested the exclusion of the well-established hockey.)

In the middle of the war boarding numbers, hardly surprisingly, had fallen, but by the autumn of 1944 numbers had topped 100. Mr. Prickett had kept contact with Canterbury, and had regularly returned to the city to interview prospective parents at the County Hotel. (Advertisements were placed in the local press in advance of his visits.) The safe situation of Truro no doubt appealed to parents, particularly to Kentish parents, who saw the dangers from flying bombs and rockets supersede the earlier dangers of invasion, bombing, or shelling. The fact that the school offered 'entire charge of boys from evacuation areas during all school holidays' must have proved an added attraction. As many as 30 K.C. boys at a time were accommodated at Tremorvah during the school holidays. Whatever the reasons, it was certainly a remarkable feat to return from evacuation with more boarders than the school had housed before the war. For the second time John Prickett had led the school to safety after a period in which even mere survival semed doubtful.

CHAPTER ELEVEN

Memories of Exile in Truro

Memories of John Prickett (Headmaster 1934-60)

At the beginning, about 50 boys slept in Tremorvah Hall and 30 in Truro School gymnasium in the care of Douglas White. Eventually we had boys sleeping in eight different houses including 'Three Corners' under Mr. Hargreaves, 'Elstow' under Mr. and Mrs. Richards, 'Belmont' under Mr. and Mrs. Gibson and 'Mrs. Beard's' – a lady who took in boys when our numbers began to increase. For, miraculously, our numbers did increase during our time in Truro. When we moved to Truro from Canterbury in May 1940 we took with us about 80 boys. By March 1943 the number had fallen to 73 boarders, though by then we had recruited 20 local day-boys. By November 1944 the number of boarders had risen to 103 plus about 20 day-boys, and from this point onwards K.C. managed to pay its way and to begin to recoup some of the heavy losses made during the first year or two of evacuation.

The Senior Schools of Truro School and Kent College (apart from the boarding sides which became independent in 1941) were run as one joint school, to the great advantage of both, since both schools were rapidly losing their younger men to the forces. One year after our arrival in Truro the two schools had lost between them 15 members of staff to the Forces and the Ministry of Supply.

In spite of these losses the bringing together of the two staffs enabled the gaps to be filled and we were able to teach all subjects on the timetable in a way which would otherwise have been impossible.

From 1942-4 Mrs. Prickett acted as Bursar (of course without any remuneration!) in addition to supervision of the domestic staff and catering. The only complaint we received from a parent about food during the war was that we gave the boys an excessive amount of Cornish cream!

In a report to the Governors in November 1944 I wrote:

From every point of view it is desirable that we should return to Canterbury at the earliest possible moment . . . . The number of boys who were at Canterbury before evacuation is decreasing each term and, if we are to re-establish the school in Canterbury with many of its old traditions, it will be necessary for us to return very soon.

I cannot leave this account of the war years without reference to the 38 Old Canterburians killed in action. On Sunday, 4 November, 1946, a Memorial Service was held in the school Chapel with a large attendance of Old Boys and some parents and friends of those who had died. A War Memorial Fund was inaugurated and this resulted two years later in the installation of the memorial organ in the Chapel. This fine organ was obtained from a Congregational Church in Canterbury which was being demolished.

Extract from a letter from Mr. S.A. Spicer

Written in 1941 to Mr. W.L. Blackshaw, past President of the Old Canterburian Club

We came down here towards the end of last May, although, in my opinion, conditions at Canterbury were really not far off normal, except that we had to make occasional nocturnal treks across the field to the air-raid shelter, which was fun enough until the novelty began to wear off with repetition. But at the same time there was a good deal of scare about troop carriers dropping squads of parachutists or even themselves making a landing on playing fields; and then came the shattering collapse of France and anywhere near the Channel coast seemed to be a veritable danger-spot for a boarding school. Parents began to show some anxiety, and we on the staff got little consecutive rest because we were hauled out for every yellow warning. So, as conditions looked like worsening, we spent a few days in hectic packing and clearing up and shifted to this remote corner of the country – and believe me – it *is* remote and exceedingly primitive. Civilisation in many of its aspects has not yet penetrated into this benighted county. It is a crude and unlovely spot. I used to teach some facts about this peninsula which I now know to be horribly false. The supposedly mild winters and all that jargon about the Gulf Stream Drift are a myth. Bitter experience has exploded them, together with Dickie's fantastic yarns about picnics on the sands on Christmas Day, as hollow falsehood. The Cornish winter can be summed up in two words – cold and rainy. Especially the latter, for the skies pour down moisture in sheets for days on end and the atmosphere has as high a humidity as that of a tropical forest. 'You will notice the abundant rainfall,' said Dickie confidentially to me one day, 'and that is why everything in Cornwall is so green.' 'Including the inhabitants,' I said, *sotto voce* and with some malice – and since then the Cornish climate has been taboo as a topic of conversation, and is now used merely as a goad with which to bait P.W.R. Most of us heartily loathe the spot, but are gradually becoming inured to it.

K.C. at Truro: C.D. Stacey (K.C. 1938-49)

The evacuation to Truro was a momentous event. What a headache for John Prickett and his staff, and yet for me the move hardly registered, except a first memory of Tremorvah as a house full of beds! Outside was an inviting adventure playground. A terrace and lawns and, beyond, rhododendrons hid a small lake. Behind the house a path led up through woods to a field that later became a football pitch, a large vegetable garden with forbidden fruit and stables. No horses, but straw lofts and rats to be hunted.

In the early days the under-elevens were housed and taught in Tremorvah and could still feel a part of K.C. The older boys must have had more difficulty with identity for their education was taken on by Truro School and they were boarded out in the town. Later some of us moved out to a bungalow called The Corners, near St. Clement's. There was swimming in the Fal estuary, rowing, fishing for mackerel, cycling with Dickie Richards and a memorable week at his home in Mousehole.

Term time came to spoil these idyllic days and at 11 one climbed the hill to Truro School. This proved the least happy time; through no fault of our hosts one felt an outsider. Yet a school that produced an England rugby captain, a famous actor and Alan Charlesworth cannot have been all bad.

Of my teachers I liked and admired in particular S.A. Spicer. There in his bed-sitter on the first floor of Senior School, always available, patient, busy about a housemaster's functions, producing those sketch-maps on his mimeograph, talking cricket, all with his own special brand of humour – Spic was for me the essence of K.C.

CHAPTER TWELVE

A public school (1945-60)

The Head returned from Truro with a plan for expansion and was rewarded immediately with an astonishing rise in numbers. As in the 1970s a Labour government, contrary to popular expectation, produced a boom in applications. The Junior School, which catered for boys from seven to 11, was rehoused at Vernon Holme in Harbledown. Even so, the boarding accommodation was bursting at the seams. The problem was alleviated, but not solved, by the purchase of outhouses at Milton House in the London Road and at the Manse in the Whitstable Road.

Immediately after the war the school was included in the Government's Direct Grant list. In 1957 Mr. Prickett was invited to become a member of the Headmasters' Conference and, with the acceptance of that invitation, K.C. became a public school. The boys could wear their boaters with a difference – K.C. had arrived.

Throughout its history K.C. has reflected contemporary social movements and the 'fifties proved no exception. Britain was moving further in the direction of a meritocracy but it seemed to want its 11-plus successes and future rulers educated along traditional public school lines. K.C. supplied that need.

During this time the school acquired a sporting fixture list worthy of its public school status. Only King's Canterbury and Tonbridge, of Kent's public schools, failed to feature in that list, regarded by so many in the public school world as a sure pointer to status. The same serried ranks of boatered boys compulsorily watching the matches of the 1st XV – some apathetic, some cheering – were to be seen at K.C. as at St. Lawrence College, Ramsgate, or at Dover College. Boarders were inspected before the day's work began and sat at set places in the dining-hall, supervised by Prefects and under the watchful eye of a top table. It was a far cry from the easy routine of Tremorvah. Town leave was strictly limited and all boys had to play some games. Speech Day guests grew more distinguished. The common room, after its virtual disintegration during the years of exile, grew greatly in numbers, its affairs strictly if kindly overseen by Dickie Richards, Spic Spicer, and Douglas White, the last two of whom were bachelors. The experiment, which was started before the war, whereby a woman teacher – Miss Holmes, now Mrs. Fraser – was employed to teach the youngest forms, and was thus a member of the common room, ended with the transference of boys aged under 11 to Vernon Holme. (Even so, Mrs. Fraser told the Editor when she visited the school in 1983 that she was expected to drink her cup of tea at break time and then quickly leave the common room.) The latter went back to being a male preserve after the Second World War as it did after the First, while the three girls who had joined K.C. before 1939, one of whom was Mr. Day's daughter, Rosemary, were not replaced.

The most notable change in the 15 years from 1945 to 1960 was the great increase in the size of the Sixth Form, and with it the transformation in the destination of the senior boys. At Truro only two or three sixth-formers a year gained Higher Certificates, while about 15 could point to School Certificate successes. Of the latter, only about half gained the magical London matriculation of five credits, with minimum pases in elementary mathematics and English language. From the 'fifties onwards more and more of the Sixth Form were proceeding to University from K.C., leaving school with three good 'A' Levels, on top of seven or eight 'O' Levels. Leaving school after the 'O' Level stage was becoming something of a rarity, instead of the norm. The science Sixth was particularly strong. The staff had grown much better qualified, with a far higher proportion of graduates who possessed good honours degrees. Entry to the school on the day side, though not on the boarding side, had become increasingly competitive. Something of the old family atmosphere of the 'twenties and 'thirties was lost. The boys' spare time activities were less simple, and less centred around nature and animals, perhaps because the Junior School had moved to Vernon Holme. Certainly there is little to make the reader of the school Magazines in the 'fifties think that K.C. was a country school, whereas the countryside had breathed continually from the pages of earlier numbers. But, by then, K.C. was surrounded by the suburb of Rough Common, reminiscent of Wembley or any other post-war suburban area.

It is typical of John Prickett's modesty that his memoir only refers to the 1950 general inspection in terms of a quotation from the school Magazine of that year. The document must surely in fact be one of his proudest possessions. It refers in the frankest terms to the situation which confronted him when he took over the school and again when it was evacuated. 'Mr. Prickett,' wrote the Inspectors, 'now sees his school more prosperous than it has ever been. This prosperity is his achievement.' They concluded, 'The school is in a sound condition. The increase in numbers – particularly of boarders – has raised problems not all of which have yet been solved. But in spite of all the difficulties of the war years the problems which were so pressing and critical in 1934 have been triumphantly solved . . . .'

When one looks at these 15 years from 1945 to 1960 in detail the general impression of unity is confirmed. Within a year of its return from Truro, K.C. had adopted the basic pattern of life and routine which it was to continue until the late 'sixties. John Prickett and some of the staff had been allowed back by the R.A.F. into a part of the school buildings at the end of July 1945. Proudly heading his Headmaster's letter to Old Boys 'Kent College, Canterbury', he reported that basically 'the buildings are not much changed and that we are very fortunate in having so little damage to contend with.' Walter Price and Jack Wallis – 'me and Jack' – who had remained at K.C. throughout the war as caretakers, and, in Walter Price's case, as 'custodian of the cricket pitch' had done their job well. Only the hockey field presented 'a sad sight'. 'There is a road running right across it in front of the pavilion, and about a third of the field has been covered with hard core so that tanks and other light vehicles could be parked upon it.'

Term started on 27 September, 1945, only a week late, and applications,, both for boarding and day places, flowed in. The Junior School was established at Vernon Holme, which the Governors had bought, together with 11 acres of land, and Arthur Gibson, Tremorvah's housemaster, became its first Headmaster. Rugby was adopted as the game for the autumn term, and a list arranged which at first naturally featured fixtures with only the 2nd XVs from King's Rochester, Maidstone Grammar, and Chatham House. The names of Messrs. Prickett, Spicer, and Crumpton still appear on the summaries of First XI cricket scores and in their averages. With the return of Douglas White from the R.A.F. the next year the pre-war nucleus of staff – Richards, Spicer, Day, Crumpton, Sidney Haynes and White – were back on duty. But a larger, much more ambitious school developed. In whatever direction you looked – academic achievement, size of the Sixth Form, variety of subjects offered, qualifications of staff, quality of fixture lists at rugby, hockey, cricket, tennis and athletics, and the range and vitality of school societies, it was a greatly developed K.C. Many of the old traditions remained, however, together with the Head's ideals and his persistent refusal to be bogged down by detail. The late P.W. Richards was to describe the surprise felt by the staff when John Prickett had asked at one of his first masters' meetings: 'Do we know what our long term policy is?' They had always regarded such a meeting as 'merely a routine to discuss routine.' The post-war school was to continue to reflect the Head's philosophy. At Speech Day 1947 he announced proudly that there were boys of 11 nations at K.C. The practice was later adopted of flying the flags of different nations from the roof of the Speech Day marquee.

In December 1947 there occurred the first of a number of school plays which were to gain for the school a high reputation for drama in the neighbourhood, when David Spencer produced *Hamlet* at the Cavalry Theatre, Canterbury. In the same term, Godfrey Evans spoke to the school of his experiences on the 1946-7 M.C.C. tour of Australia and illustrated his talks with many slides. The 1st XV's fixtures included a match with the powerful St. Lawrence, Ramsgate, with whom they drew 3-3, and next term the hockey XI were playing the first XIs of Chatham House, Dover College, St. Edmund's, and Sir Roger Manwood's.

By the beginning of the autumn term 1947 the Head was to make the comment, which sounds strange to modern ears accustomed to the assumption that bigger is better: 'Unfortunately it seems inevitable that the total number this coming September will exceed 400 . . . . We are taking steps to prevent a further increase.' Those steps were taken and the school's numbers remained much the same until the advent of coeducation, 25 years later.

It was during the 'fifties that the school's academic results began to improve dramatically, and to reach the highest standards. In the summer examinations of 1950 eight boys gained Higher School Certificates in two or more subjects, while only 13 of those who took school Certificates could claim the all-important exemption from London Matriculation. Ten years later 42 gained two or more 'A' Levels, seven with State Scholarships, and the school was winning two or three open awards to Oxford or Cambridge a year. Forty-eight boys out of the 74 who sat the General Certificate of Education at Ordinary Level gained five or more passes. No one, looking at K.C. before the outbreak of the Second World War, could possibly have foreseen such a transformation.

Throughout the 'fifties house plays were regularly produced, while a series of major school play productions continued to appear. Members of staff no longer featured in their cast lists. Alan Charlesworth's cricket and rugby sides had some remarkable results from fixture lists which were now more powerful than ever before. In 1954, his first season, the cricket team won eight out of 11 matches, drawing another two. Next year it won all ten matches, and again was undefeated in 1958, as was the athletics team. In the same year, his rugby XV lost only to a Blackheath Public Schools team. When Sidney Haynes became Headmaster of Queen's College, Taunton, Douglas White took over the coaching of the hockey XI. His teams became legendary for the thoroughness of their preparation and for the robustness of their style. The Hockey Association recognised the strength of K.C. hockey during his reign by sending down exceptionally strong teams, as Tulse Hill had similarly recognised the standing of Joe Hargreaves' coaching in the early 'thirties. In the same 1958 the Association's XI which defeated P.N.S. Haynes' hockey team contained two Cambridge University Wanderers and two Cambridge blues, two Oxford Occasionals, and one Oxford blue, one member of the English Universities XI, and J.V. Conroy, the English International. It must surely have been the strongest club side to play a school in the country that year.

Much of this sporting success was made easier by the Head's inspired decision, which he describes below in his usual modest terms, to buy Moat House and Farm. As he wrote at the time, 'This is the only suitable land near the school that is likely ever to be available, and the opportunity of acquiring it may not recur'. With a depressing lack of foresight the Methodist Board of Management refused to advance the money. John Prickett then took matters into his own hands, and arranged the purchase for £9000 of the house, 2½ acres of garden, two cottages and over 90 acres of farmland, as he explains in the next chapter. The house became the Headmaster's house and formed, until its sale in 1982, a building of more distinction and grace than any other in the school's possession. Playing fields, levelled out of the farmland, have been put to constant use ever since. Further parts of that land, which the school scarcely used, were sold for building in the 'seventies, when land prices had rocketed, and the money used to build Wesley House. Without that money K.C. could never have become a coeducational boarding school. John Prickett's quick and decisive action was as important to the future of K.C. as was Edward Pillow's generous gift of land to the College in the beginning.

So the 'fifties marched on, in the era of Harold Macmillan's 'You've never had it so good', and appears to have been a remarkably stable decade in the history of K.C. It is true that there remained much that desperately needed doing to the school's basic boarding facilities. The Inspectors had pointed to the inadequacy of the dayrooms, and had described them as bare, drab and poorly furnished. Boarders were never allowed in their dormitories during the day time, and were thus forced to spend their spare time in cheerless and over-used form rooms. This made it almost impossible for staff properly to display visual material in their classrooms with which to enliven and elucidate their subject. The daily routine displayed on the calendar of 1952 reads: 9.00 p.m. Upper School to dormitories; 9.25 p.m. Sixth Form to dormitories – times which to modern K.C. boarders would seem utterly insupportable. One can only say that on the evidence, the boys of the 'fifties seem to have been a remarkably contented and conformist generation. In September 1957 the editors of the *Kent College Magazine* sent out 330 copies of one of those questionnaires about school life so beloved of editors of school magazines. The replies elicited a degree of satisfaction with the status quo which a K.C. boy of ten years later would have found profoundly shocking. Only three boys wanted less discipline, while four wanted more.

The 'fifties atmosphere has been caught beautifully by a member of staff, Mr. M.J. Craton, writing in the school Magazine. His account stays in the mind, like an impressionist painting. He is describing one of those most extraordinary of English set pieces – Speech Day – and the year is 1956:

> Everywhere there were flowers. They blossomed everywhere as if to contrast with the unpromising skies. Roses brought in armfuls from the bursar's garden, beautifully arranged under the direction of Miss Alexander, sparkled in bowls or twinkled in posies, soaking the air with scent. Patriotic carnations, syringa and delphiniums, red, white and blue, competed with yellow and many shapes and shades of foliage.
>
> And yet it rained. A driving mist dampened the masters' procession, as it made its way to the marquee, lying like a great white whale stranded on the hockey pitch bedecked with drooping flags, Sweden and Israel and Nationalist China. It almost dimmed the annual finery of the staff: the purples and scarlets, the lemon and gold of their hoods. It rose to a drumming crescendo of rain at one stage in the speeches, testing the billowing canvas and the vocal power of the speakers.

His account is full of praise for the way in which Chuter Ede, guest of honour, and Home Secretary in Attlee's late Labour Government, rose to the occasion. Those who remember David Norfolk's Speech Day oration 20 or so years later, against a background of flashing lightning and crashing thunder, which served to make him appear even more like Moses on Mount Sinai than usual, will be allowed to doubt whether even an ex-Home Secretary could rival that later performance.

In the summer of 1960 John Prickett, after 26 years at K.C., retired at the age of 52. He had been granted a term's sabbatical leave in Easter 1959, when Roy Day took over as Acting Headmaster. A year later he resigned, believing, as he writes, that it was best both for K.C. and for himself that he 'move on'. He left behind him a remarkable record. He had revived the school's fortunes in the 'thirties, brought it back from evacuation with as many boys as before, and seen it become a Direct Grant public school. In short, he had created modern K.C., and, by his purchase of the Moat House land through his own private initiative, made later growth possible. He went, with his wife, who had supported him in so many unobtrusive ways over the years, to Finchden Manor, Tenterden, a school for disturbed adolescents of high intelligence. Later he was to work for many years for the British Council of Churches. He was succeeded by a young Malvern master, David Norfolk, an Oxford graduate and keen sportsman. A very different era began.

CHAPTER THIRTEEN

Memories of K.C. in the 'fifties

Memories of John Prickett (Headmaster 1934-60)

We were able to obtain release of the school premises by the Air Ministry only in time to begin school there in September 1945. This delay was largely due to the fact that K.C. had been used as a base for the control of fighter aircraft in south-east England. The Hall was the control room and the classrooms behind the Hall had the appearance of telephone exchanges. As the Commanding Officer explained to me, they were not going to dismantle this complicated and expensive equipment until all hostilities had ceased.

Considering they had been occupied by the H.Q. of a tank Corps and later by the R.A.F., the buildings were found to be in excellent condition, only minor repairs and redecoration being required. The playing fields were more seriously damaged and it was a major task to fill in the slit trenches and to lift all the brick rubble, on which tanks had been parked, from the first XI hockey pitch, though many willing hands made light of it.

The welcome the school received on our return is vividly illustrated by the number of boys entered for our first term back in Canterbury. We brought back from Truro 102 boarders and four day-boys. At the beginning of the autumn term we had 158 boarders and 33 day-boys. By 1949 the number of boarders had risen to 230, the number of day-boys to 150, a total of 380.

At a meeting of the Governors on 6 November, 1945, I presented a scheme for the future development of the school, showing that it was intended to carry a two-form entry right through the school making a total of approximately 350 boys in the Senior School with the addition of anything from 50-75 at Vernon Holme, our newly acquired Junior School in Harbledown. (Looking back it seems incredible that this house, the former residence of Sidney Cooper the artist, together with 11 acres of beautiful grounds, could have been bought for £7000. Unfortunately, only three years later, we had to spend more than twice that sum on eliminating dry-rot.)

This scheme of development was carried through, but raised many problems of boarding and classroom accommodation on the way. On the boarding side these were largely met by the purchase of outside boarding houses – Milton House first under Mr. and Mrs. Armstrong and then under Mr. and Mrs. Ellins, and The Manse under Mr. and Mrs. Thwaite. Three new classrooms were built and this block was completed by the addition of three further classrooms and an art room.

One interesting development, which was a trend that had been started before the war but seriously interrupted by it, was the deliberate policy of gathering into the school boys of many different nationalities. At Speech Day in 1947 I reported that there were boys from 11 different nations at K.C., including China, India, Hungary, Czechoslovakia, France, Eire, Costa Rica and Holland. This, we felt, would serve two purposes: it would contribute something to the community life of the school which would have a high educational value, and the friendships between boys of different countries made here would at least contribute something to that mutual understanding between the nations of which the world stood so much in need.

In 1947 came the death of John Hargreaves who, in his unassuming way, had given himself to K.C. for 44 years and had contributed to it more than he could possibly have known. He had retired for the first time a few years before the war, but came with us to Truro and started teaching again to help to fill the gaps left by those who had been called up. At Easter 1947 he retired for the second time to his Rough Common house, but fell ill and died only a few months later.

The following year saw the production of *Hamlet* at the Cavalry Theatre with over 50 staff and boys in the cast and a whole army off-stage working at costumes, scenery, lighting, sound effects etc. It was a heroic effort under the direction of Mr. Spencer, the culmination of at least three terms of hard labour, and will not easily be forgotten by any of those who took part, nor by some of the masters not taking part whose work was too often interrupted.

It was not until the early 1950s when the large junior forms entered after the war reached the Sixth Form that the school began to see the greatly improved academic results following the increased numbers in the second and third year Sixth. From that time onwards the number of Advanced Level passes, State Scholarships and University admissions increased year by year until in 1960 it was reported at Speech Day that 80 Old Canterburians would be in residence at universities in October and that six had gained first class degrees in the summer.

But I anticipate. In November 1950 the staff and boys had their first experience of a general inspection by a panel of His Majesty's Inspectors. The *Kent College Magazine* reports, 'they probed thoroughly into every department of school life and activities, and left with a very favourable impression, stating that the school was in a sound condition.'

It was within a few years of this period that the school lost three outstanding members of staff, two to become headmasters. In 1949 Mr. J.E. ('Jackie') Crumpton left to become Headmaster of H.M.S. Worcester after 14 years of dedicated and ebullient service at K.C.; in 1953 Mr. S.J. ('Sidney') Haynes left to become Headmaster of Queen's College, Taunton after 18 years at K.C. His contribution to the academic, dramatic, musical and sporting life of the school during that time foreshadowed his distinguished career as a headmaster which was to follow. In 1955 came the retirement of Mr. P.W. ('Dickie') Richards after 38 years at K.C. – a longer full-time teaching life than any other member in the history of the school. John Hargreaves and Philip Richards together cover more than 50 years in the life of the school and have been responsible more than any others for the sense of continuity from one generation to another. Philip Richards had succeeded John Hargreaves in 1936 as Senior Master, a position he filled with great tact and dignity.

New buildings added during the 1950's included the completion of the classroom block on the far side of the quadrangle – linking it on the one hand with the workshop block, on the other with the Lower School – and the new science block (1958) built with the help of a substantial grant from the Industrial Fund for the Advancement of Scientific Education in Schools.

Until 1949 K.C. had no Chaplain. The Rev. Bernard Sewell, who was stationed at Boughton, came as part-time Chaplain in 1949, but it was not until 1951 that the Rev. E. Bernard Hall was appointed full-time Chaplain. He was followed in 1955 by the Rev. Dr. John Newton, later to become President of the Methodist Conference, and in 1956 by the Rev. Jim Bates, later chaplain of Southlands College. If there have at times been doubts about the value of having chaplains in schools, with men such as these we had no doubt about the value of ours. These men did more than they could ever have realised to represent Christian values among both staff and boys, and to develop our understanding of the meaning of Christian community. They thus helped us to move nearer to one of the goals for which the school was founded.

One major development during the 1950s was the purchase of the Moat House and Farm in 1952 or 1953. When this came on to the market it was at once clear to me that it was an opportunity for the school which should not be missed, but neither the school itself nor the Methodist Board of Management could raise the paltry sum (as it now appears) of £9000 for over 90 acres of farmland, the Moat House with two and a half acres of garden and two cottages. I therefore wrote to a number of people to seek their help and just managed (with the help of one or two Governors and some friends and relations of staff) to raise the £9000. The house and farm were sold by auction. In a few seconds we bid up to £9000 and we held our breath. There was no further bid and the property which meant so much for the future of the school was ours. After battling with planning authorities about change of use of agricultural land we were able to convert a beautiful flat field into 16 acres of playing fields and, after rotting floors had been relaid, my wife and I were able to move into the Moat House, leaving the former Headmaster's House to be used as an additional boarding house, which then become known as the Middle School House.

In 1957 I was elected to membership of the Headmasters' Conference, and thus K.C. became a 'public school'. At that time this was thought to be a 'good thing' and it cannot be denied that this recognition brought with it a certain sense of achievement.

It was shortly after this that I began to feel that the best part of my own contribution to K.C. had already been made and that it might be for the good of both the school and myself if I moved on. Subsequent experience has confirmed my impression that few schools had a happier community life than K.C. Boys and staff worked together in so many different activities (at one point the Magazine records the existence of 17 different school societies in all of which staff and boys joined together) that they saw each other more as friends than as masters and boys. This does not imply that discipline was lax or work slack. It just means that there gradually developed a different quality of discipline in which orders and punishments played an ever decreasing role. It was, of course, a fine balance. I remember being reproved by one member of staff for allowing boys to push past me in the corridor without admonishment. Perhaps he felt 'friendliness' might easily slide into disorder and chaos, and I had to recognise this danger from time to time and tighten the reins a little. But the picture of a happy, self-disciplined community based on mutual respect is predominant in the memories of most Old Boys of that time. For this I am truly grateful.

K.C. has since moved on to become co-educational and achieve greater glories, but whenever I return I recognise something of that same quality of community life without which, whatever else it might achieve, it would no longer be K.C.

Memories of A.J. Castle (K.C. 1945-50)

Mr. Castle's father was at K.C. before the First World War and his memories are to be read in the Jubilee Book. His son is a K.C. Sixth-former at the time of writing.

The school we returned to in September 1945 had largely withstood the ravages of war. It lacked signs of routine maintenance, and there were the remains of reinforced concrete which formed the base of the aerials and dug out shelters near the pavilion. The band of teaching and domestic staff (fond memories return of Freda and Hilda, among others, who had left home for Truro with the school) had returned barely weeks before the start of term and must have done a wonderful job, for the school was ready to function as designed by the time the first boarders returned. There were signs of alien occupation; the Tuck shop had been used as a WRAF clothing store and still bore the labels of female clothing on its shelves. The dormitories, dull with their dark oak partitions and newly acquired army grey blankets, displayed the remains of pin-ups; these, in tone with the period, were well clad and portrayed in black and white. We returned (and to a surprising number it really was back again after a five-year break) in two main groups. First came those from Cornwall, and then a day or so later the larger number of new boys, boarder and day, who were between them to form the new Kent College. And to oversee them, the heroes in uniform also returned: Jackie Crumpton, Sidney Haynes, Douglas White. Roy Day, in addition to his teaching duties, was to become de facto Bursar, no easy task as we set about reconstruction.

The school also had to be reconstructed domestically at a time when the nation was going through major economic problems. Shortages abounded in everything, from food to exercise books and from electricity to heating fuels. Rationing meant careful control of food portions to ensure equality for all, and there was at least one generation of boys who were prepared to eat everything. The severe winter of 1947 led to 'prep in bed' – the only place considered warm enough in the long evenings. Despite this, the large dormitories (1 and 4) were still lit (if that it can be called) only by four 60-watt lamps to cater for the 24 boys in each. Average pocket money in the late 'forties was one and thruppence in the Third Form, rising to double that in the Sixth. But few complained, and it was sufficient for a visit to Canterbury (normally on foot) and for purchases in the Tuck shop, run by the school outfitters, Gorringes of London. It was here that John Hargreaves found yet another niche for himself in the service of the school, as its manager. Sweets were rationed, and the relevant portions of the ration card were kept in the Tuck shop; ice cream, crisps and the occasional fruit pie, although in short supply, were not, and equality of distribution became a major concern of our own Mr. Chips.

K.C. prepared boys for the rigours of life beyond school – in all respects bar two: in the aftermath of war, cadet training (led by the Headmaster himself in Truro) was shunned and the K.C. leaver found himself largely unfitted for the next stage of existence for all but a handful – national service; and K.C. remained a monastic environment – association with the other sex seemed to be regarded, at best, as unnatural.

Looking back over those five years, it is difficult to pick out specific events or activities particularly worthy of record: the labour gangs digging up the brick road, or later building the brick wall round the swimming pool; the first Speech Day when somehow parents and boys were squeezed into the Chapel and subjected to a lengthy dissertation by the guest speaker (one Professor Jessup) which went on for over 50 minutes and over the heads of most of his audience; the passing of John Hargreaves, the funeral in the chapel and the cortege with boys past and present to the cemetery beyond St. Thomas' Hill; again in the chapel, when we remembered those who had not returned, and the unveiling of the organ in their memory; of the Sunday walks to church, with boater or cap – Anglicans via orchards and fields to Harbledown and Methodists to St. Peter's; Sunday afternoons, after the compulsory letter-writing period, and walks in the Chicken Woods collecting chestnuts in season, or even through the oldest railway tunnel in Britain on the Whitstable line; the St. Lawrence cricket ground with a smattering of boys to cheer on one of their own – Godfrey Evans; the sound of Sparks Spencer's spinnet – or his gramophone, apparently borrowed from the dog of HMV fame; half terms, always at Whitsun and the first weekend of November, only long enough to make room for Old Boys in their bi-annual ritual; the day off in the spring term, armed with sandwiches and a double whack of pocket money. The memories are endless, but none more enduring than that which spanned the whole period: a dedicated staff moulding those placed under their care and shaping their future.

Years of recovery and consolidation: A.P.L. Slater

Member of staff 1951-79

There are problems facing a master trying to recall the atmosphere of the school in the 'fifties: his view must be from the staff-room door, and he is aware that he himself never suffered nor inflicted on others the thousand daily tests that being a schoolboy involves. In the private areas of their lives unseen influences dominate – territorial rights and pecking orders, and all that might be called, to mis-coin a phrase, 'les droits des seniors' can make dormitories or changing rooms into nightmares never to be forgotten. Food, or the shortage of it, achieves disproportionate importance, as do marks lost and gained, or games won or lost. While aware of all these pressures, a master should be able to see persons and events in larger and fairer perspective, and judge them from a more mature and balanced viewpoint. Let him attempt that in all humility.

For me it all began one sunny afternoon in March 1951. Canterbury lay still war-flattened east of Butchery Lane, but was, in that year of the Festival of Britain, bravely staging (if that is the word) an exhibition of the city's history in the linked cellars that began where Barratt's now stands and took you on a below-basement tour of the city. At K.C. the fields were attractively busy with hockey matches in the sunshine, and I surfaced in mid-interview to hear the Headmaster, Mr. John Prickett, asking, 'Are you a Christian?', epitomising, I later realised, the tone, ethos and set of values he wanted to see pervade the school. He further inculcated these principles by taking Sixth Form classes himself. One of the German exchange boys years later recalled one of his dicta, heard in one of these classes: 'Don't be impressed by the impressive'. The first event of the first staff meeting of the year, and the last at the final end of year meeting, were the Chaplain's prayers – a tradition that was new at least to me after some years in northern and midland grammar schools.

At that first staff meeting newcomers met their future colleagues: the 'old stagers' like Second Master Dicky Richards, urbane, courteous, cultured and a gentleman in the best sense of the word; the fatherly Roy Day; the often silent but wittily sardonic Spic Spicer ('Primus' to the staff); the incisive and amusing Sidney Haynes; the serious and mathematical Doug White who saw life, hockey and mathematics as permutations of the same game; the gentleman-farmer manqué, Freddy Fowler, and the dapper master of *le mot juste*, Walton Thwaite.

These were, for the most part, to see the decade through, though the older leaves began to fall before John Prickett himself left in 1960. Dicky left in 1955 after 38 years at K.C.; more remarkable still was Walter Price who left also in 1955 but after 55 years in the service of the school – small, tanned and wiry Walter, ready with his henchman Jack Wallis 'to tackle every job from lock-smithery to preparing a wicket' (to quote Dicky's Magazine tribute). His wages in 1900 had been two shillings a week with food; his military distinction, a Military Medal won in France in 1918. Jack Wallis left in 1958, dependable and hard-working to the end.

These two last loyal servants of the school were replaced by two newcomers who were to become, in their turn, legends in their lifetimes: by 'George' (Parham), who came in 1946 to carry around the hundreds of keys to all parts of the school, many forbidden to us lesser mortals, and to mend fuses, replace bulbs, control the temperamental heating systems, conjure out of sight several hundred trunks till end of term, mend taps, discover drains, and grumble at his multifarious tasks but never refuse to give anybody a hand; and 'Ernie' (Jefferey) who came in 1957, ruddy of countenance and rotund of figure, whose painting and decorating of K.C. never ended and even his holiday gangs of boys had to jump when he cracked the whip. And, taking over another of Walter's jobs, came Ron Want in 1952, diminutive but dynamic, to make hockey pitches that the County sides regarded with envy – quite apart from the many other pitches, squares and gardens which Ron tended with his gang of assistants, to ensure that games gave pleasure and the school looked a treat.

Those who were to see the school into the 'eighties began to gather: in 1951 Don Sutherland and APLS; in 1953 the bachelors Phil Chalcraft – to take over woodwork and fill the workshop with lithe canoes every Speech Day – and Alan Charlesworth – to take over cricket and rugger – neither knowing at the time that the stars had ordained that these bachelors should become in-laws. In 1955 and again in 1957 Gordon Rodway shook the dust of M. and S. off his feet to entertain the staffroom with an endless store of wit and to drill classical learning into all forms in the school. But many will also recall the dry and piercing verbal contributions of 'C.V.' (Stephens) and the hectoring efficiency and preliminary guttural snort of Arthur Keeling, the first man appointed specifically as P.E. and games master. Bernard Hall was the first full-time Chaplain, one of a series of splendid men who gave themselves to pastoral care and daily routines as well as unflinchingly stimulating the very criticisms which were, ironically, likely to rebound upon themselves. There were the musical contributions of David Spencer in the intervals away from the labours of teaching Latin to the uncomprehending. There was Rodney Burt with his fiery enthusiasm and abounding energy seen equally in his work with English scholars, his dramatic productions, the Scout troop and tennis; and Ray Ellins (whose wife Peggy acted as honorary, unpaid, but much-loved mother to their charges at Milton House) who showed his scholarly mind whether talking of William Gladstone or Donald Bradman, and by his attitude revealed that the quest for truth was both taxing and unending; and 'Forte' Armstrong, the sensitive organist who found the vagaries of errant youth beyond comprehension, and Peter White, the vigorous champion of the individual and of the importance of emotional development. These were the staff responsible for a decade of consolidation after the disintegrating effects of exile in distant Cornwall.

The administrative offices, too, took on staff who were to stay for the decade, if not longer. Eric Woodroffe, as smart and immaculate and meticulous as he must have been on his destroyer deck, took over from Mr. Locking as Bursar in 1955, a post he did not relinquish until 1978. Mrs. Mary Wellington, to become the repository for secrets from many sources besides the headmaster, replaced Mrs. Daltry in 1953. Miss Alexander came in 1954 and left the San after coping with several spring term epidemics that filled not only the San, but at least two of the 'barn' dormitories downstairs. Miss Miller imposed a kindly but firm discipline on Lower School while Miss Gray started the first real reform in the running of the kitchen, where her bark terrified us all but where staff and boys developed an affectionate respect for her as they got to know her better.

One gained yet another perspective on the school when one looked at the boys' names in the calendar, where a glance showed how deliberately cosmopolitan the community was, boasting as it did such a list of names as Hussain, Kalyanvala, Kiralyfi, Kotecha, Lekyananda, Pkorny, Satchu, Trivedi, Zambodla and Zyto – and I recall that the Head Boys in successive years were Anglican (Blackwell), Baptist (Telfer), Roman Catholic (Tony Hills), and Methodist-with-Jewish-forebears (Aarons), not to mention the Egyptian, Hazzan, and Nigerian, Akingbehin, who were Senior Sub-prefects during the decade.

Looking at the school as an academic institution, one saw a two-form entry classified strictly by academic ability ('streaming' was not a dirty word in those days if, indeed, it was known at all). Both streams, but especially the lower, applied themselves to work and passing examinations in a way which, laudable or not, resulted in a high pass rate in Public Examinations which, in turn, kept the number of applicants for entry high. It was a notable feature of the summer term that many of the Fifth form boarders, especially those in the lower stream, were up and working on their own over an hour before the rising bell. There was a surprising readiness to get down to work, perhaps not always in the most intelligent way but with very earnest application – and, if one can judge from progress later, age and experience added sense to that application.

Because the privilege of being a Direct Grant School also imposed the obligation to accept some 25 per cent of each year's entry free of tuition fees, the first streams were of enviable standard – and, understandably, a matter of some local discontent. Of the 69 Sixth-formers in 1956 nine gained First Class honours degrees at their universities and two became university professors.

Games were valuable to us because they revealed facets in individuals' characters that we had sometimes never suspected – and this deepened our knowledge of the boy or revealed to him a characteristic of which he was himself unaware. And so, among dozens of illustrious athletes over the decade, I recall with special satisfaction the 12-year-old who, puny in size and ill-balanced by an arm withered by polio, battled his way round the junior cross-country to come in last, to have his dogged courage applauded by all those who saw him pass the tape. At the same time, it would be churlish to forget that two O.C.'s shone even in the competitive adult judgement of the day – Godfrey Evans as the unquestioned England wicket-keeper of the decade, and G.C. Justicz rowing in the Double Sculls in the Olympic Games of 1960.

Dramatic productions were always a struggle against lack of space, being forced to become peripatetic in search of stages. In December 1947, *Hamlet* was produced at the Cavalry Theatre, despite transport difficulties, featuring F.S. Telfer as Hamlet, and, more surprisingly to later generations, the Headmaster as Claudius, Mrs. Richards as Gertrude and Freddie Fowler as Polonius. In 1949 the Rough Common Hall saw *Androcles and the Lion* as well as some variety concerts. In 1952 dining tables which had been pushed together made the stage in the dining-hall, and then began a run of plays in the Chapel, starting with an outstanding *Murder in the Cathedral* produced by Rodney Burt who had the good fortune to have in Tony Hills a very competent actor, brought up as a practising Roman Catholic, to play Becket. In 1955 plays moved on to the ingenious and elaborate folding stage structure built by Phil Chalcraft and his assistants to be erected and taken down in the gym. A fine variety of plays were produced here – *Richard III, Macbeth, R.U.R.* and Obey's *Noah* among them – and, in the later 'fifties and earlier 'sixties, a number of variety shows until the present stage was put up in the transformed Chapel in 1978.

Every day of these school years, behind the kaleidoscope of events and persons referred to above, there stalked the person of one master, always changing and yet always the same – M.O.D. (master on duty) – taken for granted but always 'there, just in case . . .'. His absence, at the Odeon that afternoon in 1938 when K.C. had its fire, stopped the film so that the cinema manager could ask that 'the master-on-duty at Kent College should go up to school immediately as it is on fire'. There is a moral in that somewhere.

In a school as self-contained as K.C. then was, it is not surprising that the duties of the non-residential staff were very similar to those of the residents. The residents were responsible for dormitory and school discipline until 8.45 a.m. and after 10 p.m., but all staff alike took turns over the 13¼-hour day remaining, Saturdays and Sundays included. It was an exhausting day.

The day began at 8.45 a.m. with the bell being rung for the school to assemble in the Chapel; then the staff and Headmaster were sent for before the lesson was read. At the end of prayers, several staff would queue up to issue their individual notices on routine matters – games' practices, play rehearsals and the like – a rather wearisome and generally humourless routine though few present will forget the occasion when the master in charge of hockey, having listed a number of details about the return of shirts and flags and general paraphernalia after that day's match, was striding down the Chapel when he recalled one omission.

Never slackening pace, he suddenly roared out, 'And balls to Stacey', to the unconcealed delight of all present.

One was expected to do prowling duties when possible, but the next ordeal was lunch which, in those days, like all other meals, was a set and formal event – all boys having to go to their particular place on a particular table in the charge of a prefect or monitor and there stand in silence until grace was said. The staff ate on top table and the Headmaster said grace before the M.O.D. supervised the dismissal in silence of table after table. It was the table prefect's responsibility to report late-comers and absentees and the occasional boy who ran away could bank on the search for him starting after the first meal he missed.

School tea was a similar trial from the M.O.D.'s point of view, and some may recall the meal which encapsulated what might be called the schoolmaster's nightmare come true. The awesome and, fortunately, short-lived housekeeper of the day had gone off duty leaving instructions that no second or third loaves were to be issued to the tables (each held 13 boys) after the first loaf had been eaten, and she locked the bread out of reach to make sure her instructions were obeyed. From the boys, foiled in their requests for more slices of their humble sustenance, the rumblings of indignation grew from small beginnings to a justifiable uproar of discontent. The M.O.D. could do little but, happily for him, the boys seemed to sense that his indignation with the housekeeper matched theirs and they quietened down when he assured them that he would be seeing the Headmaster immediately. The Headmaster came over from Moat House, equally enraged, and released from a store several tins of biscuits. The M.O.D. then had to distribute their contents to each hungry boarder he met on his perambulations round the school before and during his round of prep rooms that night.

After supper in the staff room (where one learned and exchanged all the behind-scenes gossip about staff and boys) with the resident staff, under the benign 'chairmanship' of Primus, the M.O.D. would take school prayers in the Chapel at 7.45 p.m. After second prep was over at 9 o'clock, he patrolled all the dormitories in Main School, more junior forms having gone down to Milton House and the Manse in Whitstable Road earlier. All Sixth-formers besides monitors had their lights out at 10 o'clock, and the M.O.D. left the world to darkness, the Prefects and the resident staff as he let himself out of the front door which was, in turn, locked behind him.

On Saturday nights the M.O.D. was on duty in the gym for the film (which in those days was often attended by several staff and a few wives) and for the dismissal before lights out at 10 p.m. On Sundays, when the Headmaster went to St. Peter's, there was a master present there on duty, but the M.O.D. for the day was responsible for shepherding the

38 John Hargreaves,
Assistant Master 1903-36

The Hargreaves Pavilion, opened Whit Monday 1939

40 R.A.F. aerial photograph of K.C.
after six years of war and occupation of the buildings

41 Tremorvah

42 Dining-hall in the immediate post-war period

43 Boys were encour to tend their own gar 

44 The Tuck shop, with Mr. Maple behind the counter

A Sixth Form dormitory

46 Canoeing on the swimming
bath in a canoe made
in the workshop

Swimming sports

48 Opening the Godfrey Evans scoreboard.
From left to right:
S.A. Spicer, P.W. Richards, Godfrey Evans and H.J. Prickett

49 The common room 1960, on the eve of Prickett's departure.

50 David Norfolk,
Headmaster 1960-77

51 A cricket match of the
'sixties with the recently
opened Guilford House
in the background.

Anglicans over the muddy paths across Duke's Meadow to Harbledown Church. (The organist there was known for his whim of so altering the rhythm of the hymns that the school was either left behind or ahead until, in despair, they lapsed into silence.)

Sunday afternoon for the M.O.D. started with the round of letter writing in classrooms (no dayrooms in those days) before ringing the bell at 3.15 p.m., the signal for all except Prefects to go for a walk outside the school grounds until at least 4 o'clock. Out of sight meant that they were happily out of mind. Tea followed at 5 p.m. and chapel at 6.15 p.m., presided over by the Headmaster or Chaplain but taken by an outside preacher who had probably stayed overnight with the Headmaster and preached at St. Peter's in the morning. At 7.30 p.m. junior boys went to the Manse or at 8.10 p.m. to Milton House, while the rest of the school held society meetings between 8 and 9 p.m.

The discipline the M.O.D. enforced and on which he in turn depended was more formal than it later became, aided by a certain remoteness of the 'establishment', whether staff or prefects, from those in their charge. The universal practice of calling all boys by their surnames may have contributed to this, though it certainly did not affect the general friendliness, being the accepted custom of the day; boys' initials were of greater significance and some masters, like Primus, had an uncanny remembrance of them, as many Old Boys will testify.

My own recollections are of friendliness and mutual courtesy in the old school pastime where the boys (at least up to the Sixth Form) try to get away with as much as they can while the staff counter guile with guile in trying to catch them out. The school rules seemed designed to assist this.

Bounds (**h**) boys wishing to go beyond the five-mile limit must have permission from the Headmaster;(**i**) all shops in Rough Common are out of bounds except Maples and the Post Office.

Clothing (**a**) all boys must wear school caps or straw hats outside the school grounds; (**b**) Prefects and Sub-prefects must wear straw hats in Canterbury. [The tidiness of uniform dress was in general accepted without question.]

General (**a**) the only tuck normally allowed is jam, honey etc., in 1 lb. pots, fruit and sweets. Boys are allowed a birthday cake on their table on their birthday.

Contravention of such rules as these served as satisfying acts of defiance; the risk and chance of apprehension meant each party kept a wary eye on the other, without malice either way. There was no need, should you wish to be a devil, to take to vandalism or truancy. All you needed to do was not to wear your boater down town or buy yourself a 2 lb. pot of jam.

Such corporal punishment as was given by housemasters was rare, but I would not like to answer for unauthorised punishments administered by at least some of the prefectorial body who were sometimes guilty of excessive punishments in terms of lines or worse.

By the end of the decade, a generally able, cooperative and hard-working staff had been established, all owing much to the inspiration and example of a Headmaster of whose unremitting hard work in the background we could not but be aware. Firmly established, too, was the standing of the school, and it was at this point, three years after being elected to the Headmasters' Conference, that John Prickett, only in his mid-fifties despite his 26 years as Headmaster, decided that his work in K.C. was done. With his going we would also miss the friendly presence of his wife, Nellie, whose quiet and perceptive Gallic appraisal of us all both awed and charmed us at the same time. Two years before Mr. Prickett left he had seen the opening by Professor Charles Coulson of the last of the many new buildings, the new science block, financed by parents, friends and Old Boys in addition to a substantial contribution from the Industrial Fund.

It was a school in very good heart that he handed over to his successor.

Memories of the Reverend P.N.S. Haynes (K.C. 1951-8)

The Senior School offered a secure and stable world in which to grow up. Freddie and Sparks were housemasters in Lower School and inspired an interest in rugger and the choir. Both interests blended together to the accompaniment of the smell of polish, when choir practices were arranged to take place in Chapel after a first XV home match on Saturday afternoons. The cheering that accompanied compulsory attendance by the whole school left little voice for *Aces and Galatea*, or a Mendelssohn anthem. But Miss Tilley and the girls from K.C. Pembury would arrive to change all that. And the Under-14 hockey XI took over the First XV pitch and challenged their First XI, massive mascot gollywog and all.

Academically, K.C. amalgamated some brilliant brains (usually belonging to day-boys) with some very average material. Streaming was taken for granted, and excellence rewarded with prizes on Speech Day. John Prickett established both stimulus and order in the learning process culminating once a year in the summer exams, when the gym and the woodwork shop were requisitioned and desks were spaced at suitable distances from each other to emphasise the individuality of the assignment. It was not a school for cheating or stealing (much), although one notorious Fourth Form, in 1957 I think, managed to perfect the art of shoplifting, and goods to the value of £1000 or more had to be returned to

Canterbury. But at the same time, the advent of new staff, often graduates from Oxford and Cambridge, brought new ambitions to both staff and boys, and the sizeable 1958-9 entry to Oxbridge was a tribute to those who taught us.

Christianity was presented as a life to be lived and not just a set of doctrines to be learnt. I will always remember John Prickett's sermon on Colin Wilson's newly published book *The Outsider*. We were encouraged to reflect upon what people were like and why. Resident Chaplains set the example, and the production of plays in Chapel (*Dr. Faustus* and *Murder in the Cathedral*) spotlighted the drama. Of course, there was routine religion as well. Anglicans were sent off for Morning Service at Harbledown Parish Church, and Methodists to Canterbury. The fact that this experience was so unrelated to the life of the school provided, I think, the most regular exposure of all concerned to rule-breaking and decadence. Forbidden dates with girls could be set-up for the Sunday afternoon walk. And smoking provided warmth and distraction on tedious walks in the rain. But now, as an Anglican priest, I am proud that I first received Holy Communion at the hands of a Methodist minister in the school Chapel. Of such innocence are the sophisticated arguments deployed by the stalwarts of the ecumenical dialogue born.

K.C. provided opportunity for a massive commitment to sport. For me, this made the experience of 11 years as a boarder both palatable and prestigious. In 1958 the whole hockey First XI was offered a trial for the Kent schoolboys' sides to take part in the Charles Geddes County Tournament at Seaford. The fact that the trials took place on our own school pitch was a tribute to the facilities we enjoyed, and to our groundsman Ron.

Were the seeds sown in those equable years and surroundings for the violent reactions of students in the turbulent world of the 'sixties? It is difficult to think of Kent College at that time breeding a Daniel Cohen-Bendit or a revolutionary LSE student motivated to organise the demos and sit-ins of 1968. We were protected from extremes of post-war devastation and poverty, and the purchasing-power and affluence associated with youth in the 'sixties was beyond the means of most of us. Methodist schools, like other Christian foundations, were heirs to a tradition that had stood firm through two World Wars. Christianity still offered the world a faith and a hope. We were fortunate to be educated under its influence.

Memories of Peter Gatehouse

Peter Gatehouse attended Vernon Holme and K.C. during the 'fifties and now lives in California

'Is there any boy here absent?' asked 'Dickie' Richards, white-haired and grandfatherly, unconsciously alleviating anxieties, soon to rest on well-earned laurels; 'Spic' Spicer had handwriting marvellously copperplated in an earlier age, drawn by the same undulating hand from which chalk could be directed unerringly down a loquacious throat; 'Archie' Beales, acid of tongue, could reduce any 'toad' to base elements, or precipitate fear with the crook of a finger; 'Stevie' Stevens, gown cocooning chauvinistic shoulders, would stalk into class like some huffy raven; Mr. Keeling, saying 'When I say go, go. Go! Coom back, that boy. Who told you to go?', would drown our laughter with his subsequent ire; and 'Freddie' Fowler would ever prefer to be farming in Hereford, where it was pointless to compete for his favours. My favourites, of whom appreciation has grown through the years, were 'Flapper' White, often to be observed in simple and harmonic motion on a hockey pitch, a cheerfully symmetrical figure who was instrumental in the calculation of many careers other than mine, and 'Baldy' Slater, a pippin of a man, who, with rosy cheeks and breathless phrase, brought pedantic semantics, the tricky trochee, and the melody of prose to ingenuous ears.

Out of the multitude, the names of my precursors stll evoke the awe with which they struck me then – Blackwell, Davies, Saunders, Walker, Lee – as elders and betters. Many were Prefects latterly, dispensing a justice sometimes rough, but justice nonetheless; would that the Pavilion's darker side of bullying had been more often within its boundaries.

These, characters and facets of a larger character, were the established order, an order maintained by the august, austere and authoritarian H.J. Prickett, truly the Headmaster, and rightly respected. Only after enduring years of rigid rule and the frustrations of discipline did I discern rule to be direction, and direction benevolent. I believe him to be a fine man, and it is my loss that he did not – could not – share himself more with us. Under his tutelage, direction, order and character became a matrix within which the students' own personalities and characters were fostered and drawn out.

K.C. was a society, no mere congregation of boys, established in structure and heirarchy, rich in history and myth, frequently self-policing, conservative of practice and belief, and with the highest cultural, social and sporting expectations. No one who experienced it could have caused more than a tremor in its structure, other than to enhance it with his personality, nor could any fail to be moulded by it, even though he were of Neville or Godwin. I was among the last of that era, that society; nor will its like come again. I feel privileged to have been among the loveliest and the best.

Memories of M.J. Over (K.C. 1951-8)

M.J. Over was a day-boy in the 'fifties and is now on the committee of the Old Canterburian Club

A pupil's life at Kent College seemed to revolve around rules and regulations. I have read that subjecting someone to a mass of procedures is done deliberately to develop his character. There is a danger of rebellion, of course, but with hindsight I feel that it taught one to take decisions when faced with a new situation. One did not worry others with petty questions because one was frightened to look foolish. There were a lot of very clever pupils passing through the school at this time. Day-boys had the edge because they would have had more time to spend on private study and homework. One was a member of the same group, year after year, and so one related one's progress not only in real terms but also by your relative position within one's class.

The school encouraged this by publicising class lists in every subject and also an overall list. Inevitably the 'high fliers' made all of the running, always came top and always took part in any discussion. The rest tended to just keep quiet. Adrian Slater, I recall, introduced several ideas to encourage the slower and quieter pupils.

Looking back, I imagine that the financial budgets were tight at the time and that the school had difficulty in coping with the science content of the curriculum. For instance, it only offered General Science at 'O' Level in the Fifth Form (a point always noticed by potential employers). On leaving school, I found that my science practical background was particularly weak. Note-taking in science lessons seemed endless.

School life was dominated by the competitive elements mentioned above; there never seemed any time to relax. My happiest times were in the Sixth Form, for here you were taking the subjects that you had chosen. Even English lessons took on a new dimension – the sweat of 'O' Level had passed and there was even a mixed class with pupils from another year (for the first time, some different faces!)

Under the supervision of Arthur Keeling, the school placed much emphasis on sport. I suspect that the new intake of pupils was scrutinised for potential material for a future school side. If you were good, then all was well, but, if not, then you could find yourself relegated to the 'chuckout' teams. In rugby, hockey and cricket an aimless club system prevailed whereby teams were chosen from the same group of pupils throughout the term. There was little tuition for the less able player; for instance, I was never given any lessons in cricket. Moreover, except for a few notable exceptions, there was little interest from the staff, for frequently prefects were seconded to referee or umpire games. In the summer, sport was compulsory after normal school lessons, i.e. from 4.30 p.m. to 5.30 p.m. If there was little interest from the school then it was hardly surprising that day-boys with long journeys were pleased if they found their name missing from a team list.

Another school rule hated by day-boys was that it was compulsory to attend and support first team home games for rugby and hockey. The lucky ones could gain exemption because of travelling distance, but for the rest it meant going home for lunch, grabbing a quick meal and then returning to the school on your 'half day', Wednesday or Saturday. I often wondered if the visiting teams realised that an element of the supporters were watching under duress.

The early 1950s was an era of change: many of the 'pre-war' staff were looking towards retirement and were being replaced by a younger generation; several of the latter would in turn remain at the school for many years. I feel that it was these new staff who really motivated pupils and were responsible for the high standards. Day-boys did not mix easily with the boarding pupils and were unlikely to participate greatly in school life. The classrooms and library were their domain.

I think that the subtle difference was that day-boys, even though they were outnumbered by two to one, considered K.C. as a school which happened to have boarders. The school, of course, was essentially a boarding establishment which happened to take in day-boys. Perhaps this explains why these bright pupils did not continue their association with the school after they left.

Memories of P.H.B. Cox (K.C. 1948-54)

Whatever possessed my father to incarcerate me in such a regimented world of uniformly red blanketed beds set amidst wooden cubicles, of frightful Sub-prefects and of the smoke-enveloped Freddie[24] and Sparks[25]? About two terms was the going rate to settle down and become an acceptable being in the school. During that running-in spell, one developed a degree of guile in breaking the house rules in the sure understanding that if you went too far, Sparks' hair brush or Freddy's slipper would bring a memorable blush to the cheeks. How well now I realise that those early disciplinary days, in comparatively harsh surroundings, were the earthy foundations on which I would build my future and set my standards!

'It was different when I was at K.C.' We have all heard those words, I must confess to having used them a few times during my son's[26] time at school and I wonder how much this collective record will confirm or deny them. Dare we say at least, that standards have changed since the 'forties and 'fifties? Then, meals were taken in semi-civilised fashion, and we accepted that perhaps half an hour was set aside, three times a day, for waiting, hearing Grace, serving, keeping silent and even using a knife and fork in the British fashion. On Sundays we walked to Harbledown or into Canterbury to attend church; letter writing occupied a strict part of the afternoon. We walked off the effects of lunch, dared to talk to a young lady or two and attended evening chapel. My sporting memories include being responsible for chlorinating the swimming pool; breaking the ice in May; competing against Duke of York's at Dover: capsizing a Firefly when leading in my first sailing race for K.C. in Dover Harbour; taking the school javelin record; sound Douglas White type tennis coaching that is still put into practice now; and proudly wearing Godwin house colours.

The teaching staff at K.C. seemed to be positive in their attitude that the average boy, as opposed to the high-flyer, needed to be prodded as well as guided along the path to success. A start in life, laying foundations, setting standards, establishing friendships, are some of the aspects of K.C. that can be recalled down the perspective tunnel of 30 years.

CHAPTER FOURTEEN

The years of David Norfolk's headmastership (1960-77)

The years of David Norfolk's headmastership were full of strife. Once again, K.C. reflected the national mood. For the 'sixties and 'seventies were years of battle – of student sit-ins, strikes and continual arguments between the sexes and the generations. The battles and arguments were refought, surveyed and even to some extent recreated by an army of university lecturers, journalists, and television commentators, whose words were read or heard by every Sixth-former in the land.

To this general mood of scratchy confrontation David Norfolk brought his own clearcut and definite personality. He was closely supported in all that he did by his wife and family, who were deeply involved in the life of the school, and he took great pleasure in their beautiful home at Moat House. Though arguments with staff and boys left their mark on him, David Norfolk was determined to fight for his beliefs and follow his own policies. The irony is that he entered K.C. determined to introduce changes as John Prickett had done before him, and yet soon found himself confronted with outside forces of change whose nature and power he could never have foreseen.

His first Speech Day address set the tone: 'Ours was a good school, he told us,' wrote the 1961 Magazine reporter, 'but it could be better, and we could not afford to stand still'. Or again, two years later, 'The main theme of the Headmaster's address may be aptly summarised in one word – *change*. We have all heard and read much of how the "wind of change" is blowing with various degrees of intensity through many countries and many facets of life, and obviously our school is not to be left behind in this process.'

Beside him, as he spoke on this occasion, sat the visiting speaker Dr. Geoffrey Templeman, the first Vice Chancellor of the new University of Kent. Nine years later both men must have felt at times almost overwhelmed by those winds and David Norfolk was defiantly

The School Game.

START

Go this way. As you pass Go collect your pocket money (1)	Spend all money in Tuck shop trying to impress new assistant (2)	Have no money for Chapel collection → LOSE 2 TURNS for guilt complex (3)	Have money, but still put nothing in collection ← LOSE 1 TURN for guilt complex (4)	MISS CHAPEL ADVANCE 2 SPACES (5)	LOCKER SEARCH MISS ONE TURN (6)	FOOD IN LOCKER MISS ONE TURN (7)	CIGARETTES IN LOCKER MISS 2 TURNS in lieu of rroided essay (8)	SHERRY IN LOCKER ADVANCE 2 SPACES (9)	VODKA, brandy, gin etc. in locker. Get sent to Housemaster (10)
LOSE FIVE TURNS WHILE YOU RECUPERATE FROM STRAIN OF SCHOOL LIFE (40)	DESPERATE FOR FOOD go down town BUT (12)	DEAD MAN'S ARM FOR SWEET THROW AGAIN (13)	Graveyard stew for lunch THROW AGAIN (14)	LATE UP locked out of breakfast LOSE 2 TURNS (15)	Thrown out of tea for starting to eat too early. Miss sausage roll & 2. 15 TURNS (16)	HM very kind & understanding but suspended MISS 10 TURNS (17)	HEADMASTER (knock & enter on knees) (18)	HEADMASTER MISS 4 TURNS While you comb hair, polish shoes etc, for 1st hce (19)	House master sends you to HEADMASTER (20)
✓ get caught for hatching left LOSE 1 TURN (21)	BEFORE 3.30 LOSE 1 TURN (22)	NO BOATER FINED 6d (23)	NO SCARF FINED 1d (24)	NO TROUSERS FINED £2 & PUT ON PROBATION (25)	DECIDE TO CATCH UP WITH WORK (26)	LOSE 2 TURNS FINDING BOOK (27)	LOSE 2 TURNS FINDING SOMEONE ELSE'S Book (28)	WORK → (29)	
Caught reading newspaper LOSE 2 TURNS (38)	Caught in Common Room during periods LOSE 1 TURN (37)	Learning fast! Locked in during HOUSE RUGGER. FOR QUICK THINKING ADVANCE TO 36 GO (36)	Locked in Changing Rooms during P.E. MISS A TURN (35)	TREATMENT BEASTLY — gated. LOSE 4 THROWS (34)	Caught in Rough Common during Prep MISS (33)	MAKE A STYLISH EXIT (32)	DECIDE TO TAKE A BREATH OF FRESH AIR (31)	Having seen bloodhounds called off, letting to inertia MISS 2 TURNS (30)	WORK

RULES :

1. One dice only may be used, except when one participant is a cheat.
2. The game may be played any number of times but you must finish by 17th December.
3. All rules must be observed.

Barry Parkinson

The School Game

proclaiming: 'Many young people have stopped expecting the adults around them to present them with patterns of behaviour, cultural standards and moral values, and have turned to the disc-jockeys for their culture, the hippies for their behaviour patterns, and the Rolling Stones for their morals.' The local paper headlined its report of the speech NO HIPPY CODE AT KENT COLLEGE.

In the 'sixties the turnover of staff was high. Some went in the normal course of events. Sydney Spicer and Roy Day retired in 1963, and C.V. Stephens in 1967. Freddie Fowler died in 1962 and Walton Thwaite in 1965, both in harness. Bill Anderson and Roy Smith were appointed to headships. Of the 25 names which appeared in the 1962 Red Book, 16 had disappeared by the end of the decade. Or again, of the eight members of staff appointed in the two years 1962-3 none remained by the beginning of the Christmas term, 1968. (The pace seems to have been particularly hot among music masters.) The 'sixties were years of high staff turnover in most secondary schools, but these changes left their mark on the common room. It was particularly unfortunate that hard though David Norfolk tried to establish a rapport with his Second Master, Douglas White, he never really succeeded.

As for the strife that stemmed from the national mood, much of it was concerned with appearance – with uniform, boots, and hair. David Norfolk dressed with the most scrupulous care. Like many men of his

105

generation he found the fashions of the 'sixties personally offensive, when young men wanted to grow their hair over their shoulders and delighted in wearing their tatty jeans at home on all occasions, including the most formal. Senior boys cared equally about these badges of their generation, and could see no reason why, simply because they were at school, they had to appear in a manner which set them apart from the rest of their age group. In this, Head and boys were simply fighting campaigns which were being fought with more or less intensity in every secondary school and in many homes. In the end, a compromise was reached by the mid-seventies which has lasted up to the present day. Uniform was retained in class, but personal clothes could be worn out of it. Boaters were abandoned. Hair was no longer cut 'short back and sides' and, once the fashion for very long hair had gone, boys could choose their own styles, so long as their hair was clean. By then the wheel of fashion had turned, so that by the 'eighties it is fashionable once more for young people to look smart. No one who spends a week at modern K.C. with its almost complete equanimity about pupils' dress and general appearance could believe the intensity of these battles of the 'sixties.

Of course, the war over hair and dress was an outward and visible sign of an inward disagreement about fundamentals. One by one the basic principles of the traditional boarding school system were successfully attacked by senior boys, often supported by sections of the staff. In this process Guilford, (the new boarding house built in 1964) took the lead. The prefect system and the strict division of the school population into a hierarchy of age divisions changed slowly into the present free and easy mixing of year groups, with the prefect regarded as more of a helper or an administrator than a non-commissioned officer. There was only one compulsory service on Sundays for boarders. The boarding side of life was thrown wide open. Boys could go home – if they had a home to go to and had no school commitment – every weekend. Boarders were allowed regularly into Canterbury and Sixth-formers could spend Saturday evenings 'down town'. Compulsory games for all were cut to a minimum, along with compulsory watching of First XI hockey or First XV rugby matches. The timetable was greatly widened so that a wide variety of subjects could be combined in the Sixth. Meals were served on a cafeteria basis. The day of the long table supervised by a prefect at its end was over. In its place came the atmosphere of the student canteen. Boarders no longer leapt out of bed at the sound of the rising bell, while seniors stayed up as late as they were allowed or later.

Thus the compulsory routine of boarding school life was pared to a minimum. The institution tried to do all it could to avoid being an institution. The needs of the individual were paramount. All these changes and more occurred in David Norfolk's time, chiefly towards the end of it. They didn't occur easily. They were often won in the face of the Head's original disapproval. But that the changes occurred, that they occurred without the disintegration of the school community, and that the larger school of the late 'seventies was well taught, basically if not, inevitably, universally happy and widely respected, was an achievement for which he must be given a substantial part of the credit.

At first, life went on much as before. In the Easter term, 1961, the first of the county hockey matches which were to be played on the First XI pitch in the 'sixties was held at K.C., before a crowd of 1000 people. David Norfolk singled out the school scout troop, with its 12 Queen's Scouts, for especial praise in his Speech Day address. Tony Matthews, later to play the part of Lord Lucan in an ITV production of the 'eighties, shone as Macbeth. In the school questionnaire classical music was found to be more popular with the boys than any other type of music.

In the next few years, the house system was introduced by stages[27]. With it went a substantial building plan and the opening of a Development Fund. One of the features of the former was not only the building of a new boarding house, Guilford, which was opened under Alan and Audrey Charlesworth's management in 1964, but more humble enterprises designed by Eric Woodroffe and executed by Mr. Laming, and Messrs. Sims, Jeffery and Parham, otherwise known as Arthur, Ernie and George. Buildings such as the Sixth Form common rooms, which were produced by this team, must have saved the school thousands of pounds. With the opening of the Development Fund went the creation of the Friends of Kent College, who have helped the school's development in innumerable ways.

Under Chaplains Jim Bates and Frank May, Christianity, continually embattled, showed a remarkable flexibility of response and sincerity of purpose. Frank May's organisation of a summer fete for 'Freedom From Hunger' in June 1963 produced not only £900 for an adopted village near Madras, but inspired a special magazine called *Dives and Lazarus*, conceived and executed by David Hilliam, which received a mention in the *Guardian*. At the general inspection, held in November 1962, the Inspectors were particularly struck with the school's Christian ethos. They wrote: 'Here is a Christian society and much of what is best in the school's way of life comes out of the unobtrusive but deep religious sense which unites teacher and taught, and animates a common sense of service.'

Under the directorship of Keith Carter, assisted by Neville Brown and Brian Jones, a poet whose first book of poems was well received nationally when it appeared in 1966, a number of plays and satirical reviews (the latter through the society *Scorpion*) were produced which reached the highest standards. In 1965 Keith Carter produced his first school play, Wesker's *Chips with Everything*. In 1966 he produced a miscellany on the themes of war and peace in our times, much of it written by Brian Jones – *Right Hand, Left Hand*. In 1967 he produced *Othello* and the next year *Antigone*. All these productions asked to be judged as dramatic productions in their own right, and not as school plays, and made a striking impression on those who participated or watched them being performed.

During the whole of the decade K.C. maintained the excellent academic record which had been established for the first time in the 'fifties. The school's 'O' and 'A' Level results were consistently good[28], while there was a steady trickle of Open Awards to Oxford and Cambridge. Whatever amount of change in the general mood of the school may have been occurring outside the classroom, the standards within it were maintained and improved. In 1963 one-third of K.C. was in the Sixth Form – and this at a school where 30 years earlier a Sixth Form scarcely existed. One in three boys left K.C. for university and in 1965 more than 20 boys were sitting Oxford and Cambridge scholarship and entrance papers in their seventh term in the Sixth. In the four years 1966-9 nine awards were gained at Oxford and Cambridge. The record of academic success was to continue in the 'seventies.

The 'seventies saw a series of sponsored walks for charity which not only raised large sums of money, but provided virtually the whole school with a carefree Sunday, in which boys could dress as they liked, and enjoy themselves enormously with the approval and participation of the staff. School societies struggled in the 'seventies as they had done in the 'sixties. Until the mid-seventies the records of the first teams at rugby, hockey and cricket could not compare with those of the 'fifties.

The most unusual of all school plays occurred during the autumn term of 1969. Keith Carter produced Brian Jones' *A Long Saint Monday*, a play written specially for K.C. There was a large cast and an equally large army of ancillary helpers. In the 'seventies Martin Child produced *The Thwarting of Baron Bolligrew* – a play which again deployed a very large number of actors and helpers, as did his *Royal Pardon*, and maintained the school's high dramatic reputation.

The 'seventies were the years of worker participation and of representation on boards of management. K.C. reflected the national trend with a School Council – memories of John Prickett's earlier experiments – and staff representation on the governing body. The former has faded away[29], though the latter remains. The 'seventies were also the years of increasing unity between the churches. In 1970 a joint Anglican-Methodist Confirmation service was held in the Cathedral for the first time. It was presided over by the Methodist Chairman of the District and the Archbishop of Canterbury, Dr. Ramsay. Dr. Ramsay later preached in K.C. Chapel, one of his last public engagements as Archbishop.

The miners' strikes of 1972 and 1974 directly effected every member of the school. The writer will never forget those evenings when the lights went out for periods of up to four hours on end, and boys dashed through dormitories and past flimsy inflammable partitions carrying candles. We were fortunate to avoid serious trouble.

The arguments about dress and week-end social life, about boarders' hours of going to bed and rising continued and were given a new twist when Parliament declared that adulthood began at 18 instead of 21.

With the 'seventies, the general rate of staff turnover declined, and the relations between Head and common room improved. The Head put his finger on one of K.C.'s greatest strengths when he referred, at Speech Day 1972, to the number of successes which boys achieved at 'O' and even 'A' Level, though they had been judged at the age of 11 not to be up to grammar school standard. In the same speech he pointed to the successful record of the cross-country team, which won nine out of its ten matches and was to provide the school's main sporting success in the middle of the decade. He also announced that the Governors had granted him a term of 'study leave' during the autumn term ahead and that during that time Douglas White was to be the acting Headmaster. It was already rumoured that he would spend some time touring coeducational boarding schools, with a view to introducing coeducation at K.C. when he returned.

The rumours were proved correct. In the autumn term of 1972, when numbers topped 400 for the first time at K.C., the Head visited about half of the country's 20 mixed boarding schools. At the same time the Laybourn Report was published which made various proposals, following the committee's earlier inspection of Methodist secondary schools, about their future, and made it clear that the committee favoured coeducation. In his Speech Day address of June 1973 the Head announced that the Governors had decided cautiously to move towards coeducation. In September 1973 the first two day girls were admitted – Carol Finch and Sandra Martin – into the Sixth Form. In September 1975 the first full-time and permanent female member of staff – Mrs. Wendy Lunel – joined the staff, and with her the first full intake of 20 day-girls at the age of 11. The policy of taking roughly half the annual day intake as girls had begun. The more important decision – to take boarding girls – in a school which was predominantly boarding in numbers and ethos, would depend on practical considerations for its implementation.

The governors reached their decision to go coeducational for a number of reasons. At the same time as the school moved towards coeducation it was being forced to move towards independence, through the withdrawal of the Direct Grant in 1975. If the school was to go independent it had to grow larger and approach the 600 mark. The only way this could be achieved, without a drastic fall in academic standards, was to take girls. This basically economic argument was reinforced by the general educational-cum-social argument. Increasingly, Head, staff, and Governors – there was remarkable unanimity on the matter – favoured the move on the grounds that an artificial divison of schooling on the basis of sex at the age of 11 had little obviously to commend it, except possibly the achievement of the highest academic success, and even this seemed doubtful. As for the boys, those among the seniors who expressed views about coeducation had been urging its introduction for several years. Looking to the long-term future it seemed probable that at some time in some form K.C. would seek to join the country's national system of education, and it would prove easier to merge with that system if the school was coeducational. So long as this development took place in a properly planned and deliberately conceived manner, and did so from the age of 11 – rather than admitting girls only into the Sixth Form, as was and is generally the case with public schools – there was a consensus for doing so.

It was much easier to agree on the general desirability of coeducation than it was to bring it about, particularly on the boarding side. Each scheme of adapting existing boarding accommodation, already seriously overcrowded with boys, to take girls had only to be examined to be discarded. If the school was to take girl boarders it must build boarding houses for them. Only by selling some 12 acres of Moat Farm land for building – land only occasionally used as playing fields – could the money be raised.

For 14 years the local authorities had opposed such a sale, not wanting further countryside to be lost. Now they relented, and planning permission to build was granted. Then, just when the way ahead seemed clear for the sale, a last minute hitch developed. A proposal was placed before the Board of Management for Methodist Residential Schools at its meeting in June 1973 that the money from the sale should not go straight to K.C. but that, for the moment, it should be used by the Board to help pay off some of its more pressing obligations at other schools. The proposal would have ended any possibility of K.C. becoming a coeducational boarding school in the foreseeable future.

David Norfolk heard of the proposal five days before the meeting of the Board, on which he did not sit. The Chairman of Governors, the late Professor Walter Hagenbuch, however, did. The two men launched a last-minute campaign, approaching personally as many members of the Board of Management as they could contact. By means of a most forceful presentation of the school's case, the proposal was withdrawn. Years of delay were to follow, but at least when the land was sold the school could keep the money. The introduction of coeducational boarding has changed K.C. more radically than any change since the return from Truro. Without the sale it could not have been introduced when it was. It was an achievement fit to be compared with Pillow's original gift of the land, or Prickett's purchase of Moat House and the land surrounding it.

Such debates about the future made little impact on most of the boys. They remained, as ever, more involved in immediate concerns. In March 1973 the Director of Music, Charles Everhart, presented the first of many concerts in Canterbury Cathedral. (Later the school's end of term Christmas carol services were to be held there regularly.) Throughout the 'seventies the maintenance staff were continually at work turning gaunt and bare dormitories into study bedrooms for more and more boys. Community service schemes were launched by Robin Hutt, the Chaplain, and boys went regularly to St. Augustine's Hospital, or to help the handicapped, or generally to visit those in need. John Morris' rugby XV in 1973 began the long road back to success which was to culminate in John Trotman's and David Shire's unbeaten sides at the end of the 'seventies and the beginning of the 'eighties. In 1975 Martin Child produced and wrote what he called a 'topographical revuesical', *Canterbury By Pass*, which was a little masterpiece of its kind; B.B.C. Radio Medway twice broadcast its songs. Stephen Slade and Charles Everhart combined to produce *Noye's Fludde*, and involved more than half the school actively in their production. Madrigal Group concerts, orchestral concerts, rock concerts and organ recitals were regularly performed. The Midsummer Evenings, performed in the grounds of Moat House, stay particularly in the mind. The combination of madrigals, strawberries and cream, closely cut grass, a backdrop of trees and hot June nights created an occasion of pure magic. The school magazine, by then produced only once a year, was revolutionised. Lavishly and imaginatively illustrated, with its concentration centred more on the school's creative writing and designing skills than on a record of the school year, it grew better each year. One of its numbers, that for 1975-6, gained special commendation from the judges of *The Sunday Times* School Magazine Competition.

The school's academic record of high achievement was maintained in the 'seventies. There was a modest revival in first team sport. Four of Stephen Slade's 1977 hockey XI played for Kent schoolboys and Andrew Conway later gained a full Welsh international cap. Andy Reeves made 1000 runs and took 100 wickets during his years in the First XI. The cross-country teams dominated the area and Nick Brawn went on to win five Oxford blues (a record) and international honours. When David Norfolk, who was appointed headmaster of Ashville College, Harrogate, in 1977, delivered his farewell Speech Day address he could fairly have claimed (though he didn't in fact do so) not only to have maintained the school in good health, but to have increased its numbers, improved its facilities, widened its curriculum, and launched it on a radically new course. What he did announce on that occasion was that a new boarding house for girls would be opened in 1978, designed to take 30 girls initially but 'capable of extension to about twice that number'. The four year delay that had followed the decision to sell the Moat land for building, whose story is told by John Butler in his memoir on p. 129, was over. Coeducational boarding was about to begin.

CHAPTER FIFTEEN

Memories of K.C. during the 'sixties and 'seventies

K.C. 1960-77: David Norfolk

Headmaster of K.C. during those years, now Headmaster of Ashville College, Harrogate

I came to K.C. in 1960, proud to be appointed Headmaster at the age of 33, but utterly ignorant of the nature of the task ahead. My first impression of the school as I reported to the Governors was a feeling of admiration for my predecessor, John Prickett, and for the way he had led the school through very difficult times and brought it to a level of excellence marked by his election to the Headmasters' Conference in 1957. The more I learned of the economic problems of the 1930s, the trauma of wartime evacuation, the desperate need to build up numbers of pupils after the return, the more I appreciated John Prickett's achievement. (I was reminded of John 4.38: 'I sent you to reap that for which you did not labour; others have laboured, and you have entered into their labour.')

However, it needed no great insight to realise how much remained to be done. I was frankly appalled by the shabby appearance of the school. Even the front of the school was a depressing sight, the gravel drive pitted with holes and puddles, an apology for a rose bed forming the centrepiece, bushes and stunted trees shutting out the sunlight. Inside the building it seemed as if successive bursars had known only one colour of paint – chocolate brown – and corridors and halls presented a uniformly drab sight. This was something which could be improved at comparatively little expense and, with the support of the current Bursar, Eric Woodroffe, and the invaluable help of Peter White, the Head of the Art Department, work at once started on brightening up the place. I seem to remember we invited the boys themselves to suggest a new layout for the

113

front drive, and we made extensive use of light, pastel colours to replace the dark brown on interior woodwork and walls.

It was not always easy to persuade the Governors that changes had to be made. A number of them had served the school well over many years, but they were no longer young. The Chairman himself was in his eighties and still thought of the school as it had been in his youth, a small, private establishment for the sons of Methodist ministers and laymen. I am not sure whether it was a help or a hindrance that I had spent the previous six years at Malvern College, a well-established Midlands school organized on traditional public school lines, possessing spacious grounds and impressive buildings, its prosperity owing much to the generosity of its Old Boys. Whenever in the early days I suggested the need for change at K.C., thinking particularly of its new status as a public school on the Headmasters' Conference, I was accused of wanting to turn the school into another Malvern – or Rugby or Marlborough. As Governors retired or died they were replaced with younger men active in public life and they became a great support to me and to the school.

Always one was conscious of a shortage of money. The school had no income apart from the fees paid by the parents and the direct grant from the Department of Education and Science, and since the fees were kept very low in order to attract boys from the widest possible social range there was never any money to spare for extras. In any case, the D.E.S. kept a close eye on the accounts of the Direct Grant schools, and the school could not obtain permission for an increase in fees unless need could be proved. The Bursar had to keep a close rein on all expenditure, and it is to his credit that so much was done on such a tight budget.

I think the area of school life which caused me most concern was the lack of a traditional house system. I had been accustomed to a school where the boys came together for lessons but where the rest of their time was spent as members of a boarding house of 50 or 60 boys under the care of a housemaster and his wife. At K.C. there was no such house organisation. The 'houses' were just a collection of dormitories, and as a boarder grew up in the school he moved through a series of houses: Lower School, Middle School, Upper School (with usually one year at least spent in an out-house in the town.) Since he never spent more than two years in any unit he formed no lasting attachment to any of them nor to any housemaster. In fact, the housemasters seemed to have little function other than to hand out pocket money or exeat chits, and they were rarely able to get to know a boy really well. The situation was not helped by the fact that the three housemasters were unmarried, each living in a single bedsitter. (The absence of feminine influence in the school was something which worried me very much in the early days, and thoughts of a move to coeducation may have been in the back of my mind even then.)

The day-boys were even less involved in any house loyalty except on the games field. The organisation cut across existing boarding units. I was interested to discover that when a general inspection of the school had been carried out some years before, one of the comments of the Inspector was that although Kent College was a boarding school it had the atmosphere of a day school.

To make matters worse, the boarders lacked almost all house amenities. Dormitories were simply for sleeping in, the boys had no studies and very little in the way of day rooms, common rooms or games rooms. It seemed that, for many of them, all they possessed which they could call their own was a bed in a dormitory and a desk in a classroom. My aim, therefore, was to change the house system in such a way as to improve the lot of the boarder, to appoint married housemasters, give to the housemaster much greater responsibility and, by involving the day boys also in the life and activities of the house, to produce closer loyalties and a much more satisfactory provision of pastoral care. It did not happen overnight. In fact it took 12 years to achieve.

The first step was taken in 1963 with the appointment of Mr. and Mrs. Chalcraft as housemaster and wife in Lower School, after Mr. Fowler's death. Guilford was opened in 1964, and Milton in 1967. The final piece of the jig-saw was not added until five years later when further alterations to the main building provided a splendid second floor flat for Mr. and Mrs. Henn. I firmly believe that nothing has contributed so much to the well-being of the school and to the creation of the family spirit at K.C. as the institution of this tightly knit house system.

For its success it was essential that the right men were available for appointment as housemasters. I can only say that in this I was singularly fortunate. From 1970 onwards Phil Chalcraft in Lower School, and Alan Charlesworth, Chris Wright and Brian Henn in the senior houses, formed a team on whose dedication I could count at all times and with whom I found it a privilege and a pleasure to work. I am sure that the example they set will make it easier for others to follow in their footsteps.

'When did you first think of going coeducational?' is a question I am often asked and to which it is not easy to provide a quick answer. A number of different factors contributed. In the first place I have to record that I spent my own Sixth Form years in a coeducational school, and although after five years in a traditional boys' school I found it an unnerving experience, it was there I met my wife – for which blessing I have never ceased to be grateful. As an educationalist I have never felt the force of the arguments in favour of single-sex education, and in an age in which almost all primary and higher education is mixed it seems indefensible to separate the sexes during the very years when they most need to understand each other. As a headmaster I find myself constantly

115

referring to the school as an extended family, a community in which we learn to accept each other, to respect and understand each other, as happens in any happy family, but it is a very strange 'family' which has room only for one sex. In every way, therefore, I was predisposed towards coeducation, but I do not know if I would have presented firm proposals for a move to coeducation at K.C. if it had not been for three other developments. The first was my awareness that a number of boys' public schools had started to admit girls from 1968 onwards (even though most limited this to a Sixth Form entry) and that the Headmasters' Conference was unlikely to expel any member school for taking such a step. The second was the Laybourn Report which appeared in 1972 and recorded the findings of a team of Inspectors who visited the Methodist boarding schools in this country. At that time all the schools were single-sex, but the Report strongly recommended that some of the schools should consider becoming coeducational. The third was a series of visits I made in the autumn of 1972 to coeducational boarding schools in different parts of the country. The school Governors had generously granted me a sabbatical term in which to carry out my own research. I visited schools of widely different types, some of them L.E.A. schools, some independent. I was not favourably impressed by everything I saw, but I came away convinced that if K.C. could truly be said to be a caring community this was the soil on which coeducation could thrive.

I returned to present my findings to the Governors and we began to plan the move to coeducation. We knew that in the early stages we should not have the money available to provide boarding accommodation for the girls, but we were convinced that, provided we made a success of accepting day-girls, it would not be long before there would be a demand for girls to board. And so it happened. When we accepted the first girl boarders at Vernon Holme we were consciously accepting a commitment to provide boarding accommodation for girls in the Senior School. My wife and I were proud to be invited back to open Wesley House in 1978, and delighted to know that the housemistress would be Mrs. Wendy Lunel whom I had appointed as the first full-time woman on the teaching staff three years before.

On the academic front things were generally in a very satisfactory state when I arrived. Under John Prickett the school had been producing impressive 'O' and 'A' Level results and sending a high proportion of pupils on to higher education. Under a well-qualified and devoted teaching staff it was not difficult to maintain these standards once achieved, although there were a few areas which needed building up. Chief among these was music, where Kent College seemed content to be a poor relation of its distinguished neighbour in the precincts. Things were slow to improve, and it was not until the appointment of Charles Everhart as Director of Music in 1970 that the musical talent which had been latent in the school was fostered and allowed to flourish.

Much of my time was spent with the Governors discussing the role the school might be called on to play in the brave new world being shaped by the educational planners. We were in a unique position in the direct grant world. K.C. was the only Direct Grant school in the country where the Local Authority had never taken up any of the free places the school was obliged to offer each year. Financially this had always proved a severe handicap, for the free places had to be awarded (and paid for) by the school Governors. But we now discovered the virtue of this particular necessity. We were beholden to no education authority, we enjoyed a greater measure of independence than any other direct grant school, nothing a Labour government could threaten us with would harm us.

When a Labour government was returned in 1974 – with a mandate to bring direct grant to an end – we were prepared to enter into serious discussion with the Kent Education Committee in the hope that they might yet find a role for us as a boarding school. I well remember the meeting in my study with the Chief Education Officer and one of the school Governors at which it was made plain to us that K.C. could play no part in any plans the Authority was making. It was, therefore, with a clear conscience that we took the decision to become a fully independent school. We realised this meant the end of free places and an end to the sliding scale by which day-boy parents of modest means paid little or nothing towards the fees. Henceforth our entry would be restricted to children from families able to pay the fees, although the Governors were able to finance a few bursaries each year and before long the Assisted Places scheme restored some of the benefits of Direct Grant.

Looking back on my years at K.C. I seem to have been fortunate in so many ways: fortunate in the school I inherited and fortunate to be able to hand it on to my successor without apology; fortunate in my colleagues, my Governors, my pupils and their parents. But of course it wasn't always like that. There were colleagues who were unco-operative, unreliable or just incompetent; there were Governors who seemed determined to obstruct or undermine what I was trying to do; there were parents who were utterly unreasonable and boys who drove me to distraction. But, then, no doubt there were times when they felt just the same about me. Memory has the incredible knack of recalling precisely the things we choose to remember, and I am only too happy to leave the ugly moments in the past. I seem to remember that in the late 'sixties and 'seventies a rebellious spirit was abroad, an anti-establishment mood possessed the most reasonable of students, drugs found their way into school and expulsions were a sad necessity. But we emerged from those difficult years to find that life was worth living after all, that values and standards had survived bloody but unbowed, and that strange comradeship between teacher and pupil, based on mutual respect and trust, appeared all the more valuable having been tested by fire.

Future generations looking back on these years may be tempted to see some guiding thread, some master plan being brought to fruition. If so, it was a plan known only to one Master and mercifully concealed from his servant below. For the most part one lived one day at a time, coped with crises as they occurred, made decisions on the evidence presented, not conscious of any master plan. Only in two respects did I formulate a policy and consciously scheme and plan to carry it through: one was the reform of the house system and the other was the introduction of coeducation. I am content to be judged by the success or failure of these two innovations. For the rest I was like an ancient mariner possessing a rudimentary compass and a hazy knowledge of the stars, at the mercy of the winds and tides sometimes contrary, sometimes benign, yet always knowing that another Hand was on the tiller and would see the ship and crew safely into harbour.

The years of discontent: the Reverend Frank May (Chaplain 1962-8)

K.C. in the 'sixties was a school seething with loves and hates. They were tempestuous, iconoclastic years in which a great new freedom was born. Not good years for being headmasters, certainly not schoolmasters and, least of all, school chaplains.

Ideologically we were all lost. The Headmaster, David Norfolk, manfully tried to impose a discipline for which we all suspected, and feared, the ideological basis had disintegrated. The Beatles, the youth explosion, *Honest to God*, the death of Kennedy, the apparent omnipotence of Soviet socialism and the cult of Maoism seemed to be saying that God and all the old classical values of authority, respect and civilised education were as dead as dodos. That is how it seemed then to sensitive boys, to worried staff and parents. Now, looking from the 'eighties, I am amazed at the littleness of our faith!

The trouble was that the youth explosion forced schoolmasters into a miserable pre-occupation with silly trivialities which were symbolic of much deeper things. The interminable harangues in assembly, debated in the common room, about the length of hair, the wearing of school boaters and caps in the city, the wearing of school uniform and looking decent for the sake of the school! Should a boy's hair be allowed to grow down over his collar? The excruciating triviality of it all! Speeches were made on it; punishments given for it; staff and boys went to pains to enforce it. No wonder we all seethed helplessly and quarrelled over school rules and 'the school's good name'. They were the pains of transition and I found it marvellous, recently, to find that our present coeducational K.C. is delivered from such miserable rancour.

Strangely enough, I loved it all and especially the healthy camaraderie of the common room. We were enriched by some seasoned old soldiers who were able to look upon the stormy scene with a detachment strengthened by experience. There was 'Spic' Spicer, sharp in his observation of boys and hiding an impish sense of humour under a stoney countenance! There, too, in his accustomed chair in the common room was Douglas White, a fine schoolmaster whose strength, orderliness and basic decency drew respect from the boys. He was a great friend to me. And I was more than honoured to be allowed to get to know 'C.V.' Stephens in his latter days and before his death. 'C.V.' looked on the 'sixties' turmoil with sardonic amusement. He wore a mask of cynical philosophising just as he wore his grey overalls to and from the Biology lab. Underneath was a warmhearted Cornishman, a devout believer in God, and a man capable of great affection. Before his death 'C.V.' told me that 'in spite of everything, old boy, the things that really matter don't change and haven't changed'. My locker in the common room was next to Walton Thwaite's. What a privilege that was! Walton was a charming man. He loved French and he loved the boys. How he would, with glee, and marvellous mimickry, regale a comic moment in his last lesson and send the room into helpless laughter! He would agonise for a quarter of an hour, and late into the evening, to find the right idiosyncratic phrase to sum up one small boy's work on a report. I watched Walton's increasing pallor with foreboding and his death was a tragedy for us all. There, too, was APLS – 'Apple' Slater, now retired in Canterbury and, thank God, still with us. I owe more to him than I could possibly say: his mercurial mind, his ability to divide his attention between half a dozen things and people at once, his patience with those who plod and his encouragement of those who soar and achieve. Adrian Slater is a man for whom great numbers will thank God and, I hope, many will emulate. It's impossible to speak of all the staff in my day. Many are still at K.C. of course. I think with gratitude of Alan Charlesworth, Phil Chalcraft, Gerald Colson, Laurence Lockhart, Bill Anderson, Gordon Rodway and, that most gifted and exhilarating personality who died so tragically – Neville Brown. How much my wife and I loved Neville! Linked with him very closely in those days was Keith Carter, whose company I have always enjoyed very much. He was the pricker of pomposity, the wit, the satiriser, the humaniser of us all. And there was the brilliance of Brian Jones, the stimulant of Bob Hughes and the marvellous things that went on quietly in the art room under the perceptive eye of Peter White. I don't think the boys had any idea how much of a pastor Peter was. He was, too, a true champion of the underdog and social justice.

But, I am drawn back to those dead weekends, with the school deserted by all but the resident staff. Boys alone in dreary classrooms and common rooms. The smell of a boys' common room! I HATE SUNDAYS etched on more than one desk lid or table. I had been through it myself. A single-sex school with parents abroad and no one to love or to love you. I always said that K.C. did not teach boys to love. But I think I was wrong. Some boys hated school, they hated Chapel, they hated me. As Chaplain I had my fair share of boys' complaints – boys rebelling, boys arguing, boys crying, boys wanting attention, boys screaming to heaven that they have been deserted by their parents, boys hating God. At the same time there were so many callers at the common room door in whom I could see the growth of self-confidence and faith and love. This is the secret of a school like K.C. – that in a boys' school there is a great deal of love.

Some of the things we dreamed about and longed for in the 'sixties have now become realities. Chief among these was coeducation. No one even dreamed of the marvellous transformation of the old Chapel that has now produced the modern, multi-purpose, intimate theatre. The old Chapel was dark, narrow, cramped and aesthetically oppressive. All that has gone, and now light and life have come into the Chapel. Thus, too, at K.C. in the 'eighties the masculine and feminine sides of all of us can be allowed to play their proper, natural part. It must bode well for the future.

The K.C. Scouts: Alan Charlesworth

Alan Charlesworth was in charge of a large and thriving scout group for 25 years from the mid 'fifties. The great majority of the boarders belonged to his scout group at one time or another during this time. It is impossible to assess the amount of sheer pleasure he gave them.

When a young man leaves college to take up his first appointment as a schoolmaster, the fear of a new life and nervousness of joining an unknown community are difficult to comprehend. To be invited to join a scout summer camp in the New Forest before the term began seemed a most friendly gesture and, although it rained everyday and we had to return early, I felt at home in the school from the first. Little did I know that this was a deeply laid plot to involve me in the activities of the troop for the next 30 years.

During the war, in Cornwall, the Cadet Corps took over from the scouts and it was only in the late 1940s that the troop was to start meetings again. Friday evenings soon became established as 'Scout Night' and all other school activities had to take second place to this. Dodge Ball in the gym, Town and Woods wide games and the usual round up of missing boys who, after a long search of the undergrowth, usually turned up on the Faversham road, and all the usual badge work. We were rather good at this and at one time we had 18 Queen's Scouts in residence. We built a new scout hut when the new science block demolished the old one and we went through the trauma of the change from short to long trousers and the disbanding of the 'scout hat'.

Of all the activities which scout groups carry out, camping must be the most popular and the one which boys remember most when they grow older. In the 1950s the camps were mainly in the south of England, and the New Forest – Barlavington and Rye were the favourite locations. Brampton Lock, near Huntingdon on the River Ouse, was visited twice, the attraction being the punts and canoes and swimming from the campsite. In the early 1960s we moved further afield and Cornwall proved a most attractive camping venue. We camped in Guernsey twice, the overnight crossings giving spice to the activity, and one year we camped near Cork, in Southern Ireland (before the troubles started). In 1966 I realised that the continent of Europe was easier to get to than many places the other side of England and since then most of our camps have been abroad. By this time, 80 or more boys were camping for the week after the end of the summer term. We visited Cul-des-Sacts, a village in Belgium in the Ardennes and, because we were the first English party to stay in the village since the liberation, the flags were put out and a great reception held which the whole village and the troop attended, and speeches made by the Mayor and Gerald Colson capped the celebrations. It was a very strange dinner we had that evening as the boys wove their way back to the campsite. Three times we camped in Holland, near Harleem, and then at Veere and it was at these camps that the group who eventually became known as 'the besotted Old Boys' first learnt their camping skills. Old Boys, staff (including the school Sister), parents and boys together made up a very large party and the logistics of getting everybody there and back became a challenge – we only ever 'lost' three boys and they came on the next boat.

Of all the countries visited, France was the favourite and there can be few English scout groups who have celebrated Bastille Day more often and sang 'La Marseillaise' with more gusto than ours. Who will ever forget the wide games over the sand dunes on the coast between Calais and Boulogne followed by Hugh Weeks' hot doughnuts around the camp fire, the trips to Cap Gris Nez and the celebrations and fireworks in Marquise, the sight of Dr. Sangster joining in the interpatrol sports and the annual celebration of Robin Gipson's birthday with the grandest meal ever produced over a camp fire, Harnden's fruit pies, 'dead ant' anywhere and everywhere, and the ringing shout of 'Last call for breakfast'? The last two years have seen yet another change and camps have been held in

Wales and the Lake District with the emphasis on rock climbing, fell walking and canoeing.

The scout group is alive and well and continues to be a source of instruction and fun for a large number of boys. In the last 30 years, well over 1500 boys have benefited from the pleasures and training first started by B.P. There are many members of staff and many Old Boys, some of whom have gone on to run their own troops, without whose help and enthusiasm all this would not be possible. A camp of all those past and present who have been in Kent College Scouts would indeed be a great gathering and a lively affair. One day I might try to organise it. Anybody interested?

K.C. in the 'sixties: David Lander (K.C. 1962-9)

Honorary Secretary of the Old Canterburian Club and a Governor of the School

'Either send me a pair of roller skates or come and collect me.' So wrote one homesick, disorientated 11-year-old to his parents from the old lecture room in October 1962. It wasn't K.C.'s fault. I'd never known anything like it. The first 11 years of my life had been dominated by the warmth of close family relationships and the easy-going informality of a country upbringing. Suddenly I was in a closely controlled community – not permitted an exeat for the first half term, and allowed out of the school grounds only three times a week: 'down town' after 3.30 on a Tuesday, to St. Peter's Methodist Church on a Sunday morning and, following an hour's supervised letter writing in the afternoon, anywhere but 'down town'.

I have heard it said flippantly of Sweden that if something is not illegal it is compulsory. Life at K.C. in the early 1960s, true to the public school tradition, was rather like that. Rules and routine seemed to govern virtually every legitimate activity. School uniform was of course compulsory at all times – sports jacket (brown herring-bone, navy blue for the Sixth Form only), trousers and grey shirt during the week, dark suit and white shirt (with a black tie of all things, wasn't it?) on Sundays. There was no television, but as crackling portable radios brought us the new sound of The Beatles and The Rolling Stones (who split us into supporters' camps rather like the Boat Race!) interest grew in the new fashions. I recall the decree that trousers must have turn-ups and be no narrower than 14 inches at the ankle; four or five years later the problem was with flaring.

By the mid-sixties hair was an issue. Lots of things were becoming issues. The new teenage cult was seeping into K.C. offering new attractions, imposing new pressures. Its dress, its music and its behaviour may be affectionately remembered today but they did not fit the system then. Most continued to conform but some began to twist and tug. It wasn't just a new craze, it was a new era.

Being fortunate still to make regular visits to K.C. I detect much more today a family in which all are able to feel 'at home'. The mood engenders a spirit of mutual concern that is able to withstand changes in teenage values and tastes much more easily than the rigid regime of the old days. It can have been no mean feat on the part of a dedicated and caring staff to dismantle some of that during the 1960s and to pave the way for the school of today.

Looking back, I suspect that the most significant change at K.C. in the 1960s was the introduction of the new house system. It helped to provide all of us with an important sense of belonging and, by installing husband and wife teams at the head of three of the houses at least, provided the means to create the family atmosphere in which greater flexibility could be tolerated. As housemaster of a completely new house known as Highfield before its official opening as Guilford, Alan Charlesworth was uniquely able to cultivate this. That he did so is manifestly apparent from the nick-name which I remember his house had in those early days – Liberty Hall!

K.C. in the 'sixties: Dr. Nick Sandon (K.C. 1959-66)

Now Head of the Department of Music at the University of Exeter.

To a boy from a small primary school in the wilds of the North Downs, whose education had previously been conducted by three middle-aged women, Kent College was at first a huge and daunting place. The buildings seemed enormous, a labyrinth of dark corridors and forbidden places, inhabited by deities, demi-gods and fellow mortals whose seniority and size required proper deference. I remember vividly my first Assembly in the austere Chapel, whose severity was softened only by the stained glass above the altar: the masters entering in the individual styles that one came to know so well (Douglas White, majestic and military; C.V. Stevens, enveloped in his gown like a crab in its shell; Adrian Slater, hurrying just a little, determined not to be left behind); John Prickett presiding with the sort of calm imperturbability that made his authority seem natural and unquestionable; the ritual singing of Hymn 870 ('Lord, behold/dismiss us'); the relentlessly positive recessional (surely it must have been the 'Tuba tune', whose dotted rhythms were to enliven almost every auspicious occasion during my seven years at K.C.).

My initial sense of awe diminished quite rapidly. The credit for this was due equally to Bruce Dick, my first form master (whose ability to talk naturally and without patronage to small boys did much to convince me that masters, too, were human) and to my contemporaries, whose friendliness, articulateness and tolerance seemed remarkable to one whose previous relations with his peers had not been rewarding. Thus I experienced at a very early stage the two qualities of Kent College that chiefly sustained me during my time there and that seems now to me to have been most remarkable: the excellent relationship between teachers and pupils, and the unusual amiability and smoothness with which the boys' society operated. Antipathies will inevitably arise in any community, and it is hard to avoid petty injustices and miscalculations; K.C. had its share of all these, but the impact that they made and the concern that they aroused showed just how small a share it was. It was largely, I suspect, the devotion and loyalty of the staff that held the school together during some difficult years in the early 1960s.

Although we did not realise it at the time, my generation saw changes at K.C. that were arguably at least as radical, if not as obvious, as those that have occurred there more recently. The school which we entered in 1959 was a very different place from that which we left in 1966. A lengthy chapter closed with John Prickett's departure, and soon masters who had served as long as or longer than he had begun to retire; to replace them there came a new Headmaster, wielding a new broom with what may sometimes have been regarded as an excess of vigour, and a new kind of teacher, disposed to question assumptions and conventional wisdom in ways that their elders cannot always have welcomed. The immediate effects of such changes may have been painful, but no institution should be immune from them; one of the peculiar strengths of K.C. was its ability to assimilate the best of what its staff and pupils had to offer, while imbuing them with its own tolerance and humanity. Thus that self-styled revolutionary Bob Hughes, who probably influenced me more than any other master, spent his early years at K.C. fulminating against the reaction and privilege for which he considered it to stand; but (I believe) he left the school regretfully and with a real appreciation of the pastoral function that it performed.

Some changes were less easily defined because they were more to do with the ways in which attitudes were changing in the country as a whole. A revealing and even startling example is that, whereas in 1960 the whole school was solemnly told by the Headmaster not to read the then notorious *Lady Chatterley's Lover*, by 1964 tender and impressionable lads of 16 were being encouraged to compare this novel with Lawrence's other more temperate work.

K.C. in the 'seventies: Richard Bain (K.C. 1965-72)

Now Head of English at Madeley Comprehensive School, Telford

Boarding-school life was no shock to me: after three years at Vernon Holme there were no feelings of isolation or homesickness, just the scramble and excitement of establishing myself in a new environment and seeing all my old friends in their new uniform. Those of us from Vernon Holme regarded ourselves as old hands and rather looked down on the scattering of newcomers: for them, away from home for the first time, and thrust into a community where the majority of their contemporaries had a superior knowledge of the system and firmly established patterns of friendship and prejudice, that first term must have been horrific. Even for us 'old hands', however, there was some adjustment to be made; after a year at the top of Vernon Holme, it was something of a comedown to be at the very bottom of K.C. – and there was this awful business of prefects. I resented them from the start, and I was amazed at the lack of support from my friends when I asked our dormitory prefect who he thought he was, bossing me about; thus my first detention.

There is so much to remember about that year: the long dormitory with its row of dark horseboxes; the row of white enamal sinks and nasty plastic toothmugs; Switzerland; endless games of 'Risk' and 'Monopoly'; pop music; table-tennis downstairs in the common room; Latin and French; the fight each evening to lay one's table with the best (preferably matching) cutlery; porridge (lumpy but plentiful); winning the dormitory decorations' contest at Christmas with a Canadian log cabin; Saturday night films; badges and secret societies; pillow fights; real fights; Sunday mornings . . . .

It was always a rush to get dressed and down to breakfast in time, but on Sunday mornings it was awful, for we had to wear white shirts on Sundays, and the regulations required that the collars should be detachable. The combination of lost/broken/unmanageable collar studs with the misery of fly-buttons (zips were not permitted) made Sunday mornings a nightmare. I never did master the collars, and I have memories of whole days spent with the studs pressing into my neck; fortunately the rules were relaxed after a year or so.

It must have been in my second year that a boy hanged himself. I remember the occasion with a lingering sense of guilt though I didn't know him well. A similar lingering guilt clings to my memories of bullyings. I was never bullied myself – I had a very tough big brother, and sufficient strength and wit myself to keep me out of trouble – and I don't think I ever bullied anybody else, certainly not systematically. I should like to be able to remember that I did something to help those that were

125

bullied, but I did not: whilst I was sorry for them I didn't much like any of them. I feel I ought to have liked them.

I was happy at school – very happy. I always returned from the holidays eager to be back among my friends after finding myself isolated and unknown back at home. But I was equipped for success: I was resilient, good at lessons, and good at sport; I wonder now how well the school was catering for its social, academic and sporting failures.

Guilford, the newest of all the houses, and only recently completed, was where we all aspired to be, and somehow it managed to retain a character quite distinctive and separate from the other houses throughout my time at K.C. In Guilford, the rigid stratification separating year from year was somehow relaxed. The atmosphere seemed freer, and they had privileges denied to the rest of us – access to cooking facilities for example. Whilst I was always jealous of my friends in Guilford, I never quite felt at home there.

My memories from the middle years are assorted: the printing club, and the pleasure of doing a real job well; the 'shack' – an old caravan where they did radio repairs and construction, and which fascinated me, despite the fact that I was, and I remain, electronically clueless; drama productions, especially *Othello* and *Antigone*; the film *The Bargee*, unmemorable in itself, but which occasioned a fierce moral diatribe from the Headmaster when he discovered there had been a seduction scene in it; innumerable sports matches; Sunday walks in Blean Woods; afternoons in Canterbury; lice scares; the Headmaster's apparent obsession with boots and long hair; open fields becoming building site, building site becoming university; the mad dash across the quad at 7.30 p.m. on Thursdays to hear the last 15 minutes of 'Top of the Pops' in the prep break; the building of the 'VAR Room'; hymns; organ music in chapel; chips for lunch on Fridays, and the frantic scramble for seconds; the huge copying and production network that produced mass translations of *Septimus* for Latin on Wednesdays; my housemaster reading *Samphire* and *Walter Mitty* complete with pocketa-pocketa sound effects after lights-out in the dormitory; playing cards all afternoon in the classroom; reading comics; walking into town to watch *Civilisation* at my English teacher's house.

Some of my fondest memories of K.C. are of the kitchen staff; one of the dishwashing machines had broken (reputedly drenching a teacher in the process) and pupils were drafted in to help wash-up. I established friendships in that time which were to stand me in good stead throughout the rest of my time at school. I could always rely on a kind word, and often an odd cake from the kitchen staff, and on one joyous occasion I contrived to miss the whole of Speech Day by helping to prepare cakes for tea.

My memories of the Sixth Form are tinged with sadness and a sense of incongruity. I remember the power and the pleasure of being house captain – the mathematical delight of preparing meticulous rotas for other people to follow – alongside my intense dislike of the prefect system and the desire to sabotage or abolish it. I remember the excitement and freedom alongside an almost unbearable sense of constraint. There were the house plays; the Photographic Club, the drugs' incident, when four boys were expelled for using L.S.D., or the beer incident when home-made beer was discovered concealed in the head boy's room; the squalor of the prefects' common room with its orange and purple walls and rows of empty milk bottles.

When it came to it, I was glad to leave and though in the end I came to reject so much I don't think that the system really matters. It is the kindness of individual friends and individual teachers that matters. These are my real memories, and with them in mind I cannot think of K.C. other than with pleasure and affection.

A Turbulent Decade: John Butler

John Butler was Chairman of K.C. Governors (from 1975-81)
During his period of office the school went coeducational and independent.
He presided over the school's most extensive building scheme this
century.

The period from 1972 to 1982 was probably the most momentous and turbulent decade in the school's history. In 1972 Kent College was a two-form entry, boys' Direct Grant grammar school; ten years later it had become a three-form entry, independent, coeducational boarding school. During the decade the school was served by three headmasters, three deputy headmasters, two bursars and three chairmen of governors. It acquired some handsome buildings and a new Instrument of Government. The number of teachers rose from 26 to 46, and the boarding fee increased from £855 p.a. in 1972 to £1400 in 1982. It was indeed a decade of change.

My own perspective on this hectic period was an unusual one. I became a Governor in 1972 and was Chairman of the Governors from 1975 to 1981. As Chairman, one is in a curious position. One knows a good deal of what is going on in the school, but much of what one knows has been selected and edited for you by other people. You have a little power and some responsibility, but you are not an inside member of the community. You know so much about the financial affairs of the school that the figures haunt you in your dreams, but you don't really know what it is like to teach there, or to work in the kitchens, or to be a pupil sitting in a freezing classroom on a January morning.

One of the dominant memories of my association with Kent College is of the abundant teas that the kitchen staff kindly provided at Governors' meetings. They were always a welcome break in the serious business of governing the school, but I came particularly to appreciate their value during my period as Chairman. I quickly discovered that Governors were rather less argumentative after tea, and I often used to suggest that we broke for tea in the middle of a difficult discussion, confident that the matter would be resolved in a felicitous way on our resumption.

I have warm memories of those who sat with me around the table at Governors' meetings. I had the marvellous good fortune to join the governing body when Walter Hagenbuch was Chairman. He was an extremely kind and courteous man and a very good Chairman. John Winter was the Deputy Chairman for much of this period, and twice became Acting Chairman. His knowledge of the financial world was tremendously helpful, and he, together with John Kitchin and Brian Haynes, provided a valuable link with the Old Boys. I was often struck by the patient and thoughtful way in which all the Governors discussed complex issues and the care they took in reaching major decisions. I felt part of a good team.

The staff representatives on the governing body also had significant parts to play. The first representative to attend meetings of the governing body was Chris Wright in 1973, and he was joined in 1976 by Keith Carter. The principle of staff representation was important, not only for the contributions that the staff representatives were able to make in the meetings, but also for the commitment that it symbolised towards corporate planning. There were genuine attempts to consult the staff at all stages of the development programme, and to try to heed their viewpoints and wishes on the major issues.

Looking back on this decade, I am still amazed that it all turned out so well. Change was in the air when I first joined the governing body in 1972. There were several reasons. The Headmaster at that time, David Norfolk, was deeply committed to the principle of coeducation. The birth rate began to fall in the mid-sixties and this, coupled with the rapidly rising costs of private education, indicated a period of uncertainty ahead. Moreover, the Public Schools Commission Report, published in 1968, was highly critical of many aspects of private education, and the Labour government elected in 1974 had a clear mandate to withdraw the Direct Grant. Kent College would have to be distinctively good if it was to flourish, offering variety and value for money to parents who wanted the kind of education it provided.

The catalyst was the publication in 1972 of the Laybourn Report, commissioned three years earlier by the Board of Management for

52 Scout troop of the early 'sixties with
the Canterbury District Commissioner

SOME K.C. DRAMATIC PRODUCTIONS

53 *The Russians*, with Messrs. Prickett and Spicer,
produced at Truro, during the war.

54 *Right Hand, Left Hand* (1966)

56 *Noyes' Fludde* (1975)

55 *A Long Saint Monday* (1969)

The Kiss (1982)

58 Moat House

59 The first full intake of day-girls

60 Pocket money: traditional life continues

61 The common room on the eve of David Norfolk's departure.
From left to right: (back row) J.G. Trotman, C.J. Dickinson, P.M. Clarke, A.J. Frost,
D.J. Shire, J.S. Williams, Mrs. W.E. Lunel, Mrs. B.L. Bruce, P. Sorenson;
(middle row) D.L. Allworthy, C.A. Everhart, R.C. Wright, B.R. Henn, R.J. Wicks,
Rev. R.E. Hutt, J.E. Finch, S.G. Anslow, D.J. Perkins, P.H. Sweet; *(seated)* C.M. Child,
G.D. Colson, G.A. Rodway, A.J. Charlesworth, A.P.L. Slater, D.E. Norfolk,
Commander E.V. Woodruffe, D.M. Sutherland, P.R. Chalcraft, W.L. Bircumshaw,
K.N. Carter

62 Dr. Paul Sangster,
Headmaster 1977-80

63 The common room on the eve of Paul Sangster's departure
From left to right: (back row) R.G. Grayson, Mrs. M.E. Frost, Mrs. A. Allmond,
C.J. Dickinson, P.M. Clarke, M. Barnwell, J.S. Williams, D.J. Shire, Mrs. W.E. Lunel,
P. Sorenson, Miss C.A. Finch, J.G. Trotman, F.I. Rudd, D.N. Hinch, J.M. Coles;
(middle row) Miss A.M.G. Thomas, A.J. Allott, C.A. Everhart, D.J. Perkins, S.G. Anslow,
J.E. Finch, W.L. Bircumshaw, B.R. Henn, R.C. Wright, P.H. Sweet, D.L. Allworthy,
A.J. Frost, C.S. Day; *(seated)* K.N. Carter, Commander P.S. Cotes, A.J. Charlesworth,
Rev. T.M. Willshaw, R.J. Wicks, Dr. P.E. Sangster, D.M. Sutherland, P.R. Chalcraft,
G.A. Rodway, G.D. Colson, C.M. Child

64 John Butler, Chairman of Governors
1975-81 receiving his leaving presentation
from Roger Wicks, Headmaster (1980-)

SCENES FROM MODERN LIFE

KENT
COLLEGE
FASHION
SHOW

65 The Kent College Fashion Show was presented equally by boys and girls (1983)

66 A rock concert

67 Ron Want, 'Nobby' Nutting and George Parham

68 Saturday night disco, 1980s

Methodist Residential Schools. It recommended the creation of a new coeducational Kent College, to be formed by merging the three Methodist schools in Kent into one single school on the Canterbury site. Nothing came of this recommendation because the Governors of the other two schools (Pembury and Farringtons) felt unable to accept it; but it nevertheless served as a significant landmark in the development of a coherent policy.

By 1973 the Governors had formally committed themselves to the principle of transforming Kent College into a Christian coeducational boarding school, with a three-form entry and an eventual size of about 600 pupils. Immediate steps were taken. An annual three-form entry began in 1973; girls were included in the intake into Lower School in 1975; and plans were drawn up for a new girls' boarding house at at cost of some £400,000, a figure which, with the advantage of hindsight, we can now see was inflated. Enthusiasm was high: things were beginning to happen. But then they began to go wrong. The key to further progress was the sale of part of the Moat land that John Prickett had bought 20 years earlier, for without the proceeds of the sale the new boarding house could not be built, and without the new house there could be no girl boarders. Yet somehow we could not finalise the sale of the land. First there were problems over planning permission; then there were difficulties with a prospective purchaser; then there were legal delays. Weeks of anxious waiting turned into months and then into years. Governors' meeting after Governors' meeting was filled with gloomy reports of one setback after another, and the tea breaks seemed to start earlier and go on longer. The staff became increasingly anxious and exasperated, and there was probably hardly a Governor who did not at some time despair of ever seeing girls as boarders at Kent College.

In the midst of this difficult period it became clear that the LEA had no need of Kent College as a boarding school, and that the price of becoming a maintained school would be the abandonment of the principles underlying the development programme. In November 1975 the Governors took the difficult decision that Kent College should become fully independent, and they instructed me, in communicating their decision to the Secretary of State, to convey their deep regret that the long and beneficial relationship between the school and the state should have ended in this unhappy way.

The decision to become independent intensified the need to complete the development programme as quickly as possible. I think the turning point came late in 1976 when two decisions were taken that had widespread repercussions. The first was the decision to admit girls as boarders at Vernon Holme from the following September, and to allocate resources from the existing reserves to carry out the necessary building alterations to accommodate them. The second was the appointment of Frank Lee Evans as architect to the school. His feeling for the spirit and needs of the school, combined with his sensitive understanding of the financial situation, suddenly transformed our prospects. Some of his lateral thinking was truly wonderful. We had been thinking for some time about the possibility of enlarging the Chapel, but always in terms of extending it towards the playing fields. It was Frank Lee Evans who immediately saw the possibility of turning the whole thing through 90 degrees and extending on the Whitstable Road side.

By May 1977 the ingredients of the building programme had been agreed and arranged in order of priority. The top priority was, of course, the girls' boarding house; then came a mixed package of conversions and new building work to provide additional common rooms, teaching rooms, staff facilities and a new music school; and then came the enlargement of the Chapel. The estimated cost of the whole programme was about £300,000, to be found partly from the sale of the land, partly from an appeal, and partly from a loan negotiated with the Board of Management for Methodist Residential Schools. Suddenly things were on the move again. By the summer, the last obstacle to the sale of the land had been cleared, and the appeal was launched. In November the Governors formally authorised work to start on the first two ingredients in the programme, and in the following March (1978) the decision was taken to proceed with the conversion of the Chapel.

The building works themselves were doubtless an abominable tribulation to those who worked in the school, but to outsiders like myself they were immensely exciting. The new classrooms, common rooms and staff facilities were all in use by September 1978; Wesley House was officially opened by David and Olive Norfolk in October 1978 (though it had actually been in use since the beginning of that term); the new Chapel was dedicated in January 1979; the new art block was opened in October 1980; and the Headmaster's new house was finished in September 1982. And such is the restless urge of a living institution that by the time I was succeeded as Chairman by David Riceman in 1981, plans were already afoot for another phase of growth and change.

Yet in spite of the necessary obsession with money and buildings, my memories of this turbulent decade are dominated by the people who shaped and guided it. I do not find this at all surprising, for the quality of life in a community is influenced most deeply not by its physical environment (though I do believe that is important), but by the people who constitute it. I have already mentioned the Governors, the staff representatives and David Norfolk, who was Headmaster until 1977. He was succeeded by Paul Sangster, who had the good fortune to inherit the development programme as it was nearing completion but the sad

130

misfortune to suffer ill health obliging him to resign after only three years. Yet brief though it was, Paul Sangster's period as Headmaster was a blessed one for the school, for he continually reminded us that the fullness of life is to be found not in bricks and mortar, but in our dealings with people and in the quality of our relationships with them. Roger Wicks was even more fortunate on becoming Headmaster in 1980 to inherit the completed programme, but it was a just inheritance for he had been deeply involved in all phases of it since his appointment as Deputy Headmaster in 1974.

Two of the unsung heroes of this turbulent decade were, in my view, the Bursars: Eric Woodroffe, who retired in 1978, and his successor Peter Cotes. It would be almost impossible to over-estimate the debt that Kent College owes to Eric Woodroffe. For 23 years he quietly got on with the business of administering the school, and in the years before his retirement he took on the enormous additional burden of coping with the development programme. The Secretary of the Board of Management for Methodist Residential Schools during most of this period was Dunstan Roberts, and although he was probably known personally to relatively few members of the school community, he played an absolutely central role throughout almost the entire decade in coordinating the development programme with the Board's policies. The Friends of Kent College, superbly led by Hugh Weekes and John Cranmer, grew in strength and fellowship throughout this period, providing the school with many facilities that could not be afforded from the school's own resources.

There are many others whose names ought to be recorded here, and in mentioning some I am very conscious of all those who are omitted. Yet I do not feel too contrite about this, for the charm and the attractiveness of Kent College is that it is a community of friends, not a collection of prima donnas. Those who were intimately associated with the school during its turbulent decade found life hectic, exhilarating, at times discouraging and depressing, but always a source of friendship, a focus of commitment, and ultimately a cause of pride in achievement.

Memories of Edward Tyler (day-boy, K.C. 1967-74)

It is a cold grey winter's afternoon and an inter-school rugby match is in progress on the main pitch near the water tower. To the fringe of reluctant spectators standing on the touchline the players are a blur of purposeful, violent movement; while they, hands in pockets, wrapped in scarves, wish they were back inside a warm classroom. They grow resentful at having been forced into the cold, feeling little or no loyalty towards their school – at least, none of that loyalty which includes cheering their team on to victory. A few shouts from some of my fellow day boys even go up in support of the other side (the first fifteen of our 'brother' school, Truro), but the cold dulls rebellion and most of the time is spent stamping one's numb feet in the mud, waiting impatiently for the final whistle. I can't remember the score. The match probably took place in my fifth year, at a time when we were beginning to question the rules and orders imposed on us.

School life had a few unpleasant aspects which were rooted in a public school ethic aimed at instilling loyalty and discipline. The day-boys were lucky in that they were regularly able to turn their backs on these constraints: promptly at ten minutes past four they walked out of the classroom to their parents' waiting car or queued at the bus stop, leaving most of the boarders within the school's confines.

One item of uniform which cut the K.C. boy off irrevocably from other youngsters in the neighbourhood was the boater. Stiff as a board, uncompromising, blatantly assertive (impossible to hide – it would not even fit into a briefcase), it was a symbol of the worst aspects of the public school ethic. Red book rule number so-and-so stated that it must be worn at all times outside the school. One evening I was walking home with one perched awkwardly on my head like an inverted nest (at least this was easier than carrying it) when a boy from the local secondary modern grabbed it and sent it spinning across a field. To the wearer it was an embarrassment, to the beholder an object of ridicule (also, perhaps, a threat and an object of envy, for did it not mark the wearer off as someone privileged, even though a snob with a posh accent?) It was abandoned at the end of my second year and the offensive object was ceremonially burnt (an action later much regretted when the boater became a fashionable part of one's after-school uniform).

The Kent College schoolboy was isolated in another way – from girls. Though naturally one of those very shy and very, very serious adolescents, I am sure that being deprived of girls' daily company helped me to see them as goddesses, shrines of worship instead of idiosyncratic, fallible, wayward individuals – similar in some ways to boys, in fact. Our biology teacher, Mr. Carter, went into some anatomical details, but how could a lesson on sexual (and also asexual) reproduction be applied to the nerve-racking business of chatting up a girl at a dance?

Kent College during the years 1967-74 was a school in slow, painful, and, with hindsight, amusing transition. Though my schooling spanned two decades, it was all part of the same era known as 'the 'sixties' – a time of full employment, optimism, 'flower power' and progressive ideas, particularly in education. Even K.C. began to fall under the influence.

In my third year I was elected on to a foundling body called a School Council. I can't remember it achieving anything: it had no teeth, just a rather feeble voice. But it existed – a tribute to the new ideas. I also stood as the Labour candidate in the school's first mock political election and actually polled a respectable number of votes in a predictably Tory stronghold, mainly as a result of an eye-catching Saatchi-and-Saatchi-style advertising campaign. Our long-haired English teacher, the poet Brian Jones, spoke to us about the ideas of Jimi Hendrix. When asked why he (Jimi) took drugs, he replied that everyone had their drug, be it a car or a television. Meanwhile certain pupils were discovering the pot scene at a notorious night club in the city, which was immediately placed out of bounds. One morning before Chapel a record called 'Atom Heart Mother' by Pink Floyd was played on the stereo system beside the organ. Mr. Rodway stood apparently unperturbed beside the revolving disc – after all, did it not sound *vaguely* like the usual classical music? He was our form master, and as such allowed us to decorate the classroom walls with newspaper and magazine articles. He drew the line, however, at even respectably clad pin-ups.

My schooldays were, on the whole, fairly happy ones. Kent College still retained some of the nomenclature of the public school (it had its Tuck shop and its Remove), and with it lingered traces of the public school ethic, but nothing to do us any serious harm (at least, not among my acquaintance). Neither staff nor Headmaster (Mr. Norfolk, a strong-minded but fair man who inspired respect) made any attempt to turn us into élitists. Even the fact that K.C. was a fee-paying school with a certain tradition did not make us unduly arrogant.

Let me finish with a few moments of schoolboy inspiration: singing my heart out at a hymn practice on Friday morning; peering through the school telescope at shadowy moon craters lit by a cold, alien yet fascinating light; sending up miniature, class-made, hot-air balloons from Guilford House to watch them float across the fields of Rough Common.

A View from the San: Sister Mary Anslow

Sister Mary Anslow was in charge of the Sanatorium from 1973 to 1982

When I first arrived in the San. in 1973 the school was a small, closely knit community of boys and masters, a school run with well-defined boundaries. Each moment of the day appeared to be accounted for both on school days and at weekends. I was welcomed into this community as one of the few women functioning in this male enclosure – we were a race apart – there to care for the more mundane aspects of school life, to provide a shoulder to cry on, the chance of a day off if one felt unwell, even sometimes someone with whom to share a hope or joy. In fact a glorified 'Mum' for 390 boys and occasionally masters too. It was a very happy school on the whole.

There was very little 'free' time. Even Sundays were occupied by a church service in town in the morning at St. Peter's Methodist Church. Boys wore smart Sunday suits all day, and Lower School boys wore white shirts instead of the daily grey. After a roast lunch a Sunday walk was compulsory from 2-3 p.m., whatever the weather. An oasis of peace for staff but not always appreciated by boys in wet and cold weather. Tea on Sunday was followed by a fairly lengthy Chapel service. Weekends of course were spent at school, only one exeat being allowed each side of half term. This tended to make the San. quite a busy place at weekends. A visit to the San might get you off the walk on a bad day, if Sister was in a friendly mood. There were also many minor injuries, caused by boys going through glass windows and doors without opening them first, hanging themselves during obstacle races in the woods, breaking arms and legs during wild games of unorthodox hockey, and occasionally impaling themselves very painfully on sharp projections while climbing on the roof.

Into this very structured community in 1975 came two Sixth Form girls. Soon, casuals were introduced for boys. Each pupil was allowed one set of casuals which could be worn in the evenings and at weekends on school premises. No 'way out' gear was allowed at all. Before the school accepted its first Lower School girls, a girl's uniform was decided upon. The familiar burgundy-coloured suits and blue-striped blouses were adopted after much discussion involving all the ladies on the staff at that time. We hankered for the luxury of tweed skirts and capes but financial considerations dictated something more practical.

There is no doubt that the school was widening its horizons with the entry of the girls, and a general relaxation of strict codes governing behaviour and dress followed. Relationships with staff had been very formal and although there had always been a caring attitude from the adult members of school, boys did not always find it possible to express their own emotions in a natural way. By 1982 attitudes had changed considerably and a farewell kiss from head boy to Sister in Chapel during a retirement presentation was accepted by all as a normal practice. This would not have happened a few years before.

Changes were also obvious on the boarding side. Large 'barns' gave way to study-bedrooms and lockers were no longer inspected for contraband. Boys seemed to appreciate this privilege although sometimes, when inspecting the large holes made in communicating study walls, one wondered if they missed the common free-for-all of dormitory days.

The problems of health that arose in an all-male school came basically from sport and epidemics. There were, however, other stresses on boys.

The constant emphasis on the masculine side only of their natures – that drinking and smoking and violent behaviour was all tied up with being a man, that it was not 'manly' to show any of the gentler attributes or to indeed show emotion of any kind – was very much a part of a male-dominated environment. Some boys reacted badly to this constant pressure to be tough and would find their way to the San. for a few minutes to have a weep in peace. There were always the small, sensitive boys who loathed all violent sport and for whom Tuesdays and Thursdays were purgatory to be lived through in fear and trembling. These would seek a refuge and salvation in the San. but too often the excuses proffered were not enough and they would return unhappily to take a few more bruises and falls, clutching a handful of tissues and a biscuit to fortify themselves for the fray. The coming of the girls opened up an opportunity for many boys to express the softer side of their nature without ridicule. For the younger children the give and take of brother and sister relationships made for a much more normal and family environment. For some boys and girls of course there were added problems. Making their first tentative relationship with someone of the opposite sex proved more emotionally disturbing than they had anticipated. To fall heavily in love at 14 to 15 years old and to be rejected is a very shattering experience. Without the maturity to know that, in two months' time, you will be in the middle of another *grande passion*, thoughts of suicide reign supreme. These problems with allied ones on whether to 'pill' or not to 'pill' now arose for the San. The time spent in listening and counselling increased dramatically. Communications between Sister and house masters benefited from the necessity to liaise about boys and girls and their personal problems. It helped to break down the feeling of isolation inevitably felt by the Sanatorium which was situated at the top of the old building – a world apart from the teeming life below.

The school has had many personalities who have made their contribution over the years. Others will have remembered great names on the academic side. Because a school is not a static community but has a constantly changing population, those who stay for many years stand out in the mind. I think of Mrs. Bacon, the housekeeper, patrolling her dining-room. She knew the boys by name and character and dealt with miscreants in her own inimitable way. Who does not remember 'Ernie'? The boys who enjoyed his baked potatoes, sausages and chips when they were in his 'gang' for painting in the school holidays, will surely not forget his lurid tales of smuggling and piracy on the high seas, which accompanied the culinary delights. Or George, the only man who knew all about the vagaries of Kent College plumbing, and dealt with gas leaks, floods and even cascades of sewage with his usual aplomb? No cries of distress from the San. were ever left unheeded by our friend George. We still have Mrs. Kedge on the staff – surely the longest-serving employee, who will be sadly missed when she goes: costumes made out of nothing for plays, curtains produced at will, never too busy to sew on a zip for a desperate master, or find a top hat for a play – and always a helping hand for the San in times of emergency. Her life has been spent at Kent College and we are the richer for it.

What matters most in a school is the hidden curriculum. The character-building, the understanding and caring attitude and, above all, the Christian values which K.C. seeks to inculcate in its pupils. These are the really valuable things which remain of paramount importance throughout the whole of life.

K.C. in the 'seventies: the Reverend R.E. Hutt (Chaplain 1971-8)

A school is a living community, and, if it is in any sense a Christian school, it must be caring and sensitive, and see itself including as valued and significant everyone in its classrooms and on its pay-roll. How, then, did the community fare during the changes of the 'seventies?

In many ways life proceeded much as usual. There were lessons to be taught or endured, exams to be prepared for, fixtures to be played; there was the kaleidoscope of concerts and outings, crises and panics, tears and laughter, frustration and satisfaction, discipline and commendation, which make up the life of most schools. The changes involved everyone and, despite all the arguments over plans and changes in long-cherished routines, we held together well, and, most important, the care for individual boys, and, subsequently, girls, continued.

Of course, as in most closely knit institutions, we had the ability of making mountains out of molehills, and I got sucked into that process along with everyone else. From the perspective of the big, outside world, the 'hair and boots' purge seems to come under that heading, as did other debates about uniform, though on the positive side it brought out a commendable *esprit de corps*, and not a little ingenuity, from the persecuted masses. To see Andrew West, with hair apparently bobbed short one day, going up to receive his Speech Day prize on the next with locks flowing to the shoulder is something I'll not forget.

But what was it all for – the drive to keep going, to maintain our character and identity after the withdrawal of the Direct Grant, to open our doors to girls, and to maintain close links with the Methodist Church, which at times was not totally happy to have us in the family? It took me some time to find my own answer to that question, as I had to work through a difficult settling-in period within an institution which seemed able to function just as well without you as with you.

Eventually I came to feel, and still do, that as a school we were there to provide as wide-ranging opportunities as we could for young people to realise and develop their potential, in an atmosphere of caring security and mutual respect. As a specifically Christian school I hoped that its members would leave knowing what Christianity was really about, rather than the caricature of it that most people seem to have, so that if they accepted it they knew to what and to whom they were committing themselves, and if they did not feel able to accept it they would at least hold it in respect, so that their minds remained open. I hoped that that would come through the classroom, where it is important for R.E. to be seen as a subject worthy of academic study and respect, and it was gratifying to see people taking the very demanding 'A' Level Religious Studies examinations. I also hoped that everyone would experience something of the qualities of a Christian community in the school's inner life and in its worship.

The farm provided an extra dimension that few schools could have matched, and the therapeutic as well as educational contribution of John, Sheila, and Peter Finch and the animals deserves an article to itself. One caveat must be entered, however, and that is that, despite the considerable number of girls, Kent College remained essentially a boys' school to which girls were also admitted. It needed more than the addition of netball and needlework to the timetable. Maybe evolving into a fully integrated coeducational school takes longer than we imagined, or it could be that not enough members of staff had sufficient experience of such schools to make it work quickly. But as far as pastoral care was concerned we were all part of a team, which included linen ladies, cleaners, Sanatorium staff and groundsmen as well as those having a more obvious pastoral function.

We were able to share in a wide range of worship: the regular Free-church type of Sunday service, quiet communion services, ancient monastic services in the series of Lenten Complines, services prepared and conducted by the pupils, with the Cathedral Carol Service and the Passion Service with its procession of cross and candles, chalice and patten, providing high-points in the year. The rebuilding of the chapel forced us to improvise with house services, early morning communions in the Pavilion (wonderful on summer mornings), and a service 'in the round' in the gym.

The most direct opportunity for Christian teaching came in training for Confirmation, yet that was always difficult and unsatisfactory. One learns the faith and grows towards commitment most commonly through the fellowship of a local church, and for Methodists at any rate, Confirmation involves membership of a local church. Such experience was rarely possible for a boarder.

Another important element within the religious aims was the

encouragement of community service. It was never easy to find enough of the right kind of opportunities for this, but work on the wards of the local psychiatric hospital, and visiting the elderly and bousebound, gave some of our young people valuable experience and insights. The same could be said of the collections and walks for charity. At least the school was aware of a great range of human need and of the imperative of Christian faith to give practical help.

There were occasions when the spontaneous love and generosity of the pupils was very moving. The way in which the school community gathered round Martin Vie as he struggled with cancer, and the atmosphere of the Sunday service the day after his death and of the funeral in the school Chapel indicated a depth of feeling, of compassion and of soul-searching that we sometimes lost sight of beneath the surface of daily routine.

I look back at those seven years with pleasure, despite times of pain and frustration. I owe a great deal to the boys and girls who peopled its classrooms and playing fields, and to the staff of all sorts who provided moments of delight and laughter, amongst whom my own education was deepened, and who suffered my mistakes with good grace. Let no one pretend that Kent College is a perfect institution, but, at the end of the day, I feel I could justify its continuing existence, could wish that it were available to all without cost, and would have been more than happy for my own children to have come under its influence and teaching.

Housemastering in the 'seventies: Christopher Wright

(Christopher Wright was housemaster of Milton House from 1968 to 79)

If I close my eyes and think of our life in Milton, I don't see a picture in my mind. I hear a bell. The housemaster's flat which Eric Woodroffe designed – single, convenient, with one large and beautiful downstairs sitting room, looking out through great windows across the school field to the water tower – contained an upstairs study. From this one gained direct access to the boy's quarters. Outside the study there's an electric bell which, in term time, started ringing around 7.30 in the morning and continued till 11.00 at night or later. Since the kitchen and sitting room are on the ground floor we found ourselves continually running up and downstairs to answer it.[30].

There on the door step would stand a boy, aged 13 to 18. The younger boy would probably supply the first ring of the day, the older certainly the last. They would be on our doorstep because the Linen Room was locked and they wanted a clean shirt, because they wanted to catch the morning post and had forgotten to draw an air letter or stamp at the proper time, because they wanted to drop out of an 'O' Level French course or join a

Chemistry course late, because the prefect had insisted that they play for the House League team but they wanted to go out for lunch with their mother who had just returned from Kuwait, because they had injured their hand playing hockey and needed an X-Ray at the hospital (that would take an hour and a half out of a busy day), because Smith was missing from tea or Jones couldn't take prep supervision, because a study holder wanted a new bulb for his table lamp, because Robinson hadn't appeared in his dormitory on time, or because (last ring at night, if you were lucky) the house was all present and correct. They were largely unimportant and sometimes unnecessary calls on one's attention (in the case of nervous new boys the unnecessary rings were sometimes concealed cries of distress) but upon these unplanned encounters depended the all-important contact which is the life-blood of housemastering. Good housemastering depends on frequent rings of the bell.

Our home in term time became something of a railway station and it was often hard on our children that it did so. On Friday evenings there would be boys dressed in every sort of disguise, blackening their faces in front of our bathroom mirror, before roaming round Canterbury on a Scout wide game. Some nights, before 'lights-out', the juniors would troop down the stairs in their dressing gowns to eat baked potatoes stuffed with sardines, to chat with my wife, and to inspect the latest batch of kittens. (Our old cat, Budge, produced a steady three litters a year for the last half of our time in the house, with four or five kittens to a litter.) Sometimes I would read a story to them in the flat or in their dormitory. (Boys' tastes are amazingly conservative, and the safest standby was always Sherlock Holmes.)

Our system had one basic premise: Milton, for two-thirds of the year, was the only home our boys possessed. Of course it was not the same as a proper home. Of course the comparison couldn't be pushed too hard. But the basic question that must be asked by a conscientious housemaster was that which must be asked by any conscientious parent: 'Would I encourage/allow/stop my own child to do such and such?' The basic assumption of a traditional housemaster in a traditional English boarding school is very different. It is: 'Here is my house. This is the way it is run. It is your duty and privilege to fit into it.'

We believed that the atmosphere of the house would come from the presence and dedicated interest of a team – from the house tutors, from the head of house and his prefects, from the linen room ladies, from the cleaning ladies, and from my wife and myself. Only by casual contact could those most in need of help, the lonely, the unliked, the different be spotted, and it is by his treatment of those boys that a housemaster who dares to call himself a Christian humanist should be judged. Only in this way could some track be kept of a group of adolescent boys, whose

139

access, in that building of a hundred exits, to a city teeming with teenage life at a time of national teenage explosion, was virtually free. It was a far cry from the established and traditional society of the boarding house at Aldenham School which I had previously run, but it provided the contact I sought.

Every house needs a series of communal efforts which will bind it together and give it a separate identity. House leagues fulfilled these purposes. They were refereed with tremendous panache and an aristocratic disdain for the niceties of the law by Keith Carter and Don Sutherland. Another source of pleasure and enthusiasm for the boy who wasn't particularly skilled at games was the athletics' standards competition, which was very much of a going concern when we took over the house. But it was the inter-house drama competition which produced the most enthusiasm in Milton. During our time there were nine productions of steadily increasing ambition produced, in accordance with the rules of the competition, entirely by a Sixth-former or occasionally by a pair of Sixth-formers. (The rows in which the Hocken twins engaged over their joint production of *The Visit* made awesome listening.)

Preparation for the production began at the beginning of the Easter term, and extended over eight or nine weeks. If, as happened on several occasions, heavy snow lay on the playing fields for half that term and more, so that the only outside activity which could occupy our 60 brave lads was invading St. Edmund's or repelling their boarders in return, rehearsals were even more of a blessing to a beleaguered housemaster than was normally the case. In Tim Pocock's production of *Zigger Zagger*, for instance, virtually the whole of one year group formed a football crowd. They played up to their role with tremendous enthusiasm, shouting, chanting, and swaying on imaginary terraces. They rehearsed for hour after hour and produced a performance of such coarse and full-blooded adolescent vitality that few of them will ever forget it. In the end, house plays went the way of the house standards competition, but I will always mourn their loss.

It is not generally recognised how much schools like K.C. contribute to satisfying national needs – the needs of those who, for a variety of reasons, require boarding school education, and thus qualify for financial help if they obtain it. Most boys and girls in independent boarding schools are there because their parents pay high fees for their attendance. Most of them could perfectly well attend local day schools. When I first looked through the Milton boys' personal files it soon became obvious that this was not the case at K.C. During most of my time in the house I, along with other housemasters, was required by the Public Schools' Commission to make an annual return, listing boys who were in need of boarding in terms of local authority categorisation. The parents of these boys could claim public help in the payment of their fees. There were ten such categories. In 1970, 40 boys out of the 61 in Milton came within one of the ten categories, and the proportion remained constant in the 'seventies. In 1979 the numbers were 46 out of 61, and their particulars were as follows:

Sons of British nationals, living abroad	3
Sons of foreign nationals, living abroad	4
Sons of members of H.M. Forces	21
Sons of parents whose method of employment is itinerant (e.g. Foreign Office, or oil companies)	8
Sons from single-parent families	8
Sons of parents, one of whom is chronically sick	2
	46

Our time ended one hot July night in our little garden at the back of our flat. We gave a party for any Old Boy of Milton who cared to join us with his wife or girlfriend on the evening of Speech Day 1979. About 100 people came. The roses which my wife had trained up against the white wall of the neighbouring art room gleamed in the night, and their scent filled the hot air. We sat there, drinking white wine, and trying, with so many familiar faces around us, to recall some of our shared experiences, before they vanished into the general blur of the past.

The life of a housemaster's wife: Helen Wright (Milton House 1968-79)

The Linen Room was to become my base in Milton House. It was a spacious room with a large, solid table of Victorian design, recently covered with cheery red Formica. Round the walls were rows and rows of square cubby-holes or shelves in brown wood with a name written on masking tape on each.

There was an atmosphere of order in the Linen Room due to the influence of Mrs. Betty Laming who had a splendid system for the collection and redistribution of laundry. Clothes hardly ever got lost and Betty could be seen, term in, term out, behind her sewing machine, repairing the irreparable, taking in trousers or letting them out according to fashion and putting patches on blue jeans.

At intervals during the day this room was turned into a diner as the Linen Room ladies had their lunch and dinner breaks. These repasts were invariably interrupted by boys seeking 'lost' clothes or giving their tailoring orders, or asking for bread. Each boy was allowed one slice at break and rushed off to toast it on one of the Heath Robinson appliances in his appropriate common room.

The main common room was where they watched T.V. It was furnished with the most fascinating collection of auction sale armchair bargains, ranged around the polished floor in a neat semi-circle.

It was a recurring sight: a large boy press-ganged by me carrying down a sagging chair. I would be bringing up the rear with a leg in my hand, to plead with Arthur, the carpenter, to put it on again. Sometimes he would – sometimes he wouldn't. He had a 'shop' behind George's yard, smelling nicely of new wood, with shavings and sawdust on the floor, and the implements of his trade neatly lining the walls.

Reporting repairs was a large part of my life. I was constantly descending the dark and murky stairs that led to George's cellar where he dispensed plastic tooth mugs, bath plugs, cup hooks and, indeed, anything under the sun. He invariably managed to come up with something for that particular emergency as we stood alongside the thumping boilers.

For larger items I had to go to a very different place – the Bursar's Office – and get a 'chit' for curtain material or for 'new' auction sale armchairs or carpets. This was a sunny, airy room with large windows fringed with Virginia Creeper. There was an old metal safe let into the wall which Commander Woodroffe would unlock. He would then extract some money from it and hand it to me as if it hurt him. He had a very military bearing but I think we saw eye to eye on 'make do and mend' and appropriate technology.

When we arrived in 1968 the permissive age had not yet influenced the rules of Millton House. Boys were not allowed in their dormitories in the day. This meant that the cleaning ladies had a pretty clear run. We planned to make it more homely and changed that rule, which meant that it was inevitably less tidy, so I had to go before the ladies to see that their task was not made too difficult. This I continued to do for 11 years. It certainly brought me in contact with the boys (for better or worse!) Our contact ranged from 'Pick up that sock!' to politics and religion. On the whole, this duty was a pleasure to me; the boys were amenable and the ladies were cheerful, hard working and humourous. I think a sense of humour was the most important quality required of a cleaning lady.

As the 'sixties rolled into the 'seventies, the pressure for privacy grew, and a great programme of partitioning into studies took place: carpets were laid and pin-ups were allowed. The latter caused some worry but some sort of compromise was arrived at. Radios and record-players were permitted and each innovation brought its own negotiation over rules. After starting off in 1968 rebuking a boy for having a Marmite jar in his locker by his bed ('I have confiscated your Marmite; please collect it from me and keep it in your common room'), I reached the situation ten years later when one boy had a dismembered bicycle under his bed!

During this period personal clothes were introduced and this meant changing after lessons into jeans and T-shirt. It also meant that lockers built for 'regulation' clothes were now bulging with fashionable garments – suede jackets and the like.

The inter-house play competition which took place each Easter term was the most marvellous example of spontaneous creative co-operation; a salutary lesson in real responsibility for the producer and a welding together of all sorts of skills in the boys, from making a recording of an eery creaking door to painting dish-cloths silver for chain mail. I used to love helping them with their costumes and props; many were the times when our flat was denuded of furniture for the sets of house plays. After the performance, the cast and helpers would come back euphorically to the flat for orange juice and crisps.

I inherited one tradition from Mrs. Winterbottom (my predecessor) and I was grateful to her for initiating it. She used to sit in the Linen Room on Friday nights when the boys came to collect their 'Bundles' of clean clothes, and I carried this on – they used to trickle in, in twos and threes, at different times in the evening, starting with the Fourths when the others were still in prep. It was a good way of getting to know people and later on the room became the centre for arguments and discussions. Like all such occasions, once they become institutionalised, they had their peaks and declines but were nevertheless very worthwhile.

Of course there were nasty moments and sometimes whole nasty terms but they righted themselves. At times one felt embattled, but then there was always the support of my husband and the Headmaster, the cameraderie with the other staff, with the house tutors, other housemasters and their wives, with Sister Anslow and the kitchen staff. My overwhelming feeling about Kent College is one of affection for all concerned and a memory of drama unlimited. We used to try to have all the boys to supper in twos or threes at least once during their time in the house but most of my contact with them was on their own ground.

In our last year when the Chapel was undergoing transformation into an all-purpose Assembly Hall, we had house Sunday services in the school Library with coffee afterwards. I even preached a sermon: it was an alarming experience.

We had foisted on us from the kitchen the excruciating nightly job of doling out orange juice and biscuits. The whole House was present, elbowing their way towards the sticky liquid – I felt I ought to be there occasionally as it took place in the hallowed Linen Room. I used to pour the drinks out and try to keep order. On one occasion, one Stephen Biggs was holding out his blue tooth mug while I poured the juice. I seemed to go on pouring for longer than the usual tot when I noticed sparkling eyes around me. There was a hole neatly bored in the bottom of the mug and the tray below was an orange wash.

On the other hand, some boys were so quiet you had to drag things out of them. One Charles Anderson was knowledgeable about birds, a subject in which I was particularly interested. I was driving him to the hospital when he was about 14. I thought I recognised a brambling on a hedge from the drawing in my bird book. I said, 'I think that was a brambling.' Silence. 'It looked like the picture in my book. D'you think it could be?' 'No'. Stung, I persisted, 'Why?' 'Because at this time of the year they are beyond the Arctic Circle.'

A dormitory prefect had put up a notice in French by the light switch: N'OUBLIEZ PAS D'ETEIGNER L'ELECTRICITE. Very neatly underneath was printed in another hand: NEIN UNTERHOSEN GRUMMEL PIMMEL ARSCH SCHLESMUSCLE DANKE. Such incidents bore one along amid the drudgery.

Then there was the eerie, dreamlike feeling of the sudden quiet at the end of term when 'the silence surged softly backwards'. Inside, in one traumatic day, beds were stripped and litter swept up as the faithful band of Linen Room ladies gritted their teeth for the long spring clean.

After that I remember moments very near to bliss, especially in the summer holidays. The beautiful games' field was bathed in sun and there was nothing but the birds and the trees to keep us company. There was time for leisurely exchanges with Audrey Charlesworth or Mary Anslow when we were able to laugh about things that were far from laughable at the time.

Our little garden behind the house was a great pleasure to me, though Ernie used to be scornful of the dog daisies and nasturtiums that ran riot there. Rambler roses grew all the way round. Surrounded as it was by three walls and a high fence it seemed, in summer, like an extra roofless room. It was there that we held our farewell party with our present leavers and Old Boys from far and wide. The roses gleamed palely in the mid-summer night. It is one of my best memories.

K.C. in the 'seventies: Mrs. Wendy Lunel

Member of staff from 1975-81, first housemistress of Wesley House (1978-81) Deputy Headmistress of Wellington School, Somerset (1981-4), and Headmistress of Stover School, Newton Abbot, from September 1984

When I joined the staff of Kent College in 1975 I stepped blithely into a situation which seemed entirely natural and sensible without any preconceived ideas of what lay ahead. I was somewhat surprised to find that the staff roughly divided into two sections – those who staunchly insisted that little girls were simply little boys in skirts, and those who held their breath in anticipation of the budding Miss Worlds who were about to lighten the corridors with sparkling eyes and swinging hips. There were many who dreaded the advent of women teachers too, as they would undoubtedly fill the staff room with geraniums and checked curtains and leave their knitting in chairs to spear the unwary. My failure to recognise the trauma of the change in Kent College tradition allowed me to find much amusement in the reactions of senior boys, who were distinctly puzzled as to why girls should be allowed to join the school at all and could only accept the idea in the belief that imminent financial collapse had forced the governors to take the ultimate, back-to-the-wall, desperate decision. The first year of co-education proved, in fact, a very easy one. The principal cause of irritation was the effect of what might today be termed a policy of positive discrimination in the reporting of sports results by the Headmaster who delivered blow by blow accounts of Under-12 netball and hockey fixtures but gave long-standing rugby rivalries and triumphs scant mention. This did nothing to endear the 20 girls to the 400 boys.

As the girls started to move further up the school, however, and to change rapidly from childhood into adolescence and womanhood, the implications and problems of a school changing from single-sex to coeducation became more obvious. Curriculum, teaching methods, discipline and attitudes of seniors to juniors all required adjustment and were being dealt with by staff who in many cases had spent most of their working life in one familiar pattern. Even matters such as whether girls and boys should be called by surnames or Christian names assumed a vital importance and, when the girls' boarding house was opened, the differences in viewpoints and disparities between attitudes in each of the boarding houses became crucial.

At times it seemed there was a loss of direction; perhaps a reflection of what was in fact occurring in society at large. Were we trying to create a unisex pupil who should be dealt with and taught in exactly the same way whether it bore the name Mary or Martin? Or were we creating a community in which the juxtaposition of opposite sexes throughout their adolescence merely re-enforced the stereo-typed sex roles of each, since neither was able to withstand peer group pressure which dictated what a girl or boy should be, and staff were unsure how to present alternatives to these stereotypes?

There were many moments during this time when I felt a real and deep anger over attitudes both amongst staff and pupils; attitudes which allowed Thursday games afternoons to be awaited eagerly as the opportunity for gazing at briefly clad sportswomen or as the occasion for flaunting a good figure to a captive audience, or which allowed the anomaly of day-girls becoming honorary members of boys' boarding houses whilst never seriously considering a reciprocal arrangement

145

whereby boys should be assigned as honorary members of the girls' boarding house. There also seemed very little opportunity to assess the longer term goals and how to achieve them by the free exchange of opinions.

In retrospect, the solutions came, however, in the very way one should have hoped; from the pupils themselves. Gradually, there was a situation in which those seniors who could be expected to assume leadership could no longer remember a time without girls or women teachers. The tensions of unfamiliarity fell away and those capable of leadership took on their roles with a composure, ability and humour that swept away prejudice and lingering doubts. The school had made the transition from a self-conscious grouping of 'boys' and 'girls' to a community of individuals, each of whom had been provided with a common social and academic life, who could go on to use their unique talents to deal with issues both within and outside the school with a better understanding of themselves and of each other.

I am sure that Kent College at the start of the 1980s was a more robust and realistic community that it had been at the start of the 1970s. I doubt that the stresses and strains of coeducational education cause the staff any less worry. I also doubt whether parents find the presence of both sexes in the school any more reassuring when considering the future of their offspring. That there were failures must be recognised. There were certainly those who got sidetracked into missing vital opportunities by their inability to balance their emotional and academic development, but the large majority of those who were educated during this transition seem now to be dealing successfully with an increasingly stressful society, with the kind of adaptability and sense of purpose which it has always been the aim of the school to develop. Coeducation thus becomes merely one more strand in the very familiar pattern of Kent College, and in which I feel privileged to have been involved.

CHAPTER SIXTEEN

Postscript (1977-84)

Paul Sangster came to Kent College as Headmaster in September 1977 from a background soaked in Methodism and Methodist education. He was the only son of Dr. W.E. Sangster, one of the outstanding evangelists of his day, and for the last ten years had been principal of Balls Park College of Education in Hertford. He had not taught full-time in a school, however, for more than 15 years.

He inherited upheaval. In one way he was fortunate in his inheritance, but in other ways he was not. The basic decisions concerning boarding coeducation and the building programme connected with it had been made. But they brought with them an atmosphere of general instability.

The building programme was the most substantial since the move across the Whitstable Road from Hoathe Court. As in the mid-thirties, builders and the sounds of their work were everywhere. The disruption caused was at its worst during morning Assemblies. With the Chapel out of action, the school met by age groups in the dining hall, where the Head often found it difficult to make himself heard above the noises of lunch preparation from the kitchen or the revelries of study holders above.

It is more difficult to define the upheaval caused by the introduction of boarding coeducation. It coincided with a fourth year's intake of day-girls at 11 and the consequent raising of the total number of girls to well over 100 – a boy to girl ratio of something under 4 to 1. For the first time, even the most uninterested or conservative boy could hardly fail to notice the presence of girls in the school. It is hardly surprising that the new situation and the generally heady atmosphere it created disrupted the lives of some boys and girls, though many others went imperviously on their ways. The most worrying aspect of that time was the imbalance of age between the sexes. There is little to be said generally for the association of boys aged 17 or 18 with girls aged 12 or 13. School discos were particularly fraught occasions. Very large numbers attended, and it

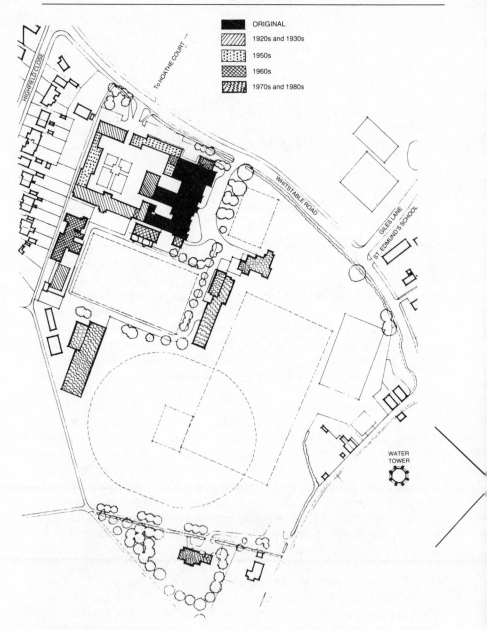

ORIGINAL

1920s and 1930s

1950s

1960s

1970s and 1980s

HIGHFIELD CLOSE

To HOATHE COURT

WHITSTABLE ROAD

GILES LANE

ST. EDMUND'S SCHOOL

WATER TOWER

100 years of expansion – how K.C. has grown

proved at first difficult to prevent the introduction of alcohol into the school. By 1980 the atmosphere had relaxed. There were increasing numbers of women on the staff, while the male staff grew slowly more at home in the new world. Boys and girls accepted each other more easily.

In the autumn of 1977 the school achieved its greatest academic success. Twelve boys and one girl, the first to do so, gained places at Oxford and Cambridge. Five won open awards. Though drama was inevitably interrupted by the rebuilding of the Chapel and the dismantling of the gym stage, two musical performances at this time were outstanding. One was the performance of two works by Benjamin Britten which christened the new Chapel in February 1979, and the other was a performance of *The Messiah* in the Cathedral. John Trotman's production of *Palach* in the summer of 1980 gripped the audience in a particularly terrible contemporary manner. The rugby teams of 1979 and 1982 were unbeaten while the 1983 XV won every match. The 1980 hockey team lost only two out of its twelve matches. The 1984 XI concluded an outstandingly successful season by defeating Kingston Grammar School, one of Britain's best-known hockey schools.

During the autumn term of 1979 Paul Sangster had been forced by ill health to rest. At the beginning of the 1980 summer term he announced his resignation. He said that though he was 95 per cent fit, K.C. needed a Head who was a 100 per cent fit. After a quiet year he took up the post of Chaplain at the Methodist girls' boarding school, Hunmanby Hall. He left behind him a school of 550 boys and girls, a new art block, a stable staff, and a gentler atmosphere. As he and his wife 'flitted' – to use one of his favourite words – out of K.C., we were left with the memory of a kindly, compassionate personality, deeply committed to his own vision of the Christian faith. He was succeeded by Roger Wicks, Deputy Head for the last six years, who had borne more than his fair share of responsibility during Dr. Sangster's last year. During his time as Deputy he had been particularly successful in widening the curriculum, and had spent hours of patient, detailed work in planning the building programme. Don Sutherland became Acting Deputy until Jo Robson took up the Deputy Headship in September 1981. John and Sheila Finch had taken over Milton two years earlier.

Roger Wicks had an unrivalled knowledge of the school's mechanics, and he was able to put his knowledge to good effect from the time he took over. There was none of the usual interim period which occurs in a school while a new Head sums up his school and begins to plan future policies. He believed that K.C. needed a period of consolidation, after the changes of the 'sixties and 'seventies. This did not stop his planning with the Governors a substantial development programme, whose first fruits will appear in time for the school's centenary in 1985. At the time of writing a

149

large new school library is being built; a sports centre should follow. K.C. has accepted places under the Assisted Places scheme and, true to its tradition of trying to help those in need of boarding, has tried to use them not only for day pupils but for boarders. Numbers have stabilised around the 570 mark. At the beginning of the Christmas term 1983 there were 575 pupils: 295 were boarders, 54 of whom were girls; 280 were day pupils, 120 of whom were girls.

The Sunday Times again picked out K.C. pupils for special commendation. This time it was a first-year Magazine for 1981-2. The judges particularly liked 'the healthy scepticism it displayed'. The phrase has an authentic ring of K.C. about it. At this time the school had once again the good fortune to experience a play specially written for its pupils. Mike Barnwell wrote a Passion play *The Kiss*, performed at Easter 1982, and later presented productions of *Saloon Bar, Macbeth* and *The Crucible*. K.C. had re-entered its former path of full-blooded and original productions. Athletics thrived with an enthusiasm which had not been seen for years, while the school played regularly in the local table tennis league, the first time, to the author's knowledge, it had done so. The boys' and girls' tennis teams in 1981-2 were outstanding, the former being unbeaten, and the latter losing only one match. By then girls' sport was as keenly contested as that of the boys.

There was no particular cause of strife between the authorities and the Sixth Form. At K.C., as throughout the country, the fear of unemployment clouded Sixth-formers' minds, and there was little interest in the battles of the 'seventies. The old issues were dead; new ones were as yet unborn. Idealism was generally regarded with scepticism.

One matter of major policy remains as yet unresolved. Coeducation has certainly arrived. Almost every form has some girls in it, and the numbers in the 'A' streams approach equality between the sexes. The intake of girls has ensured the maintenance of academic standards and brought about an extension of the school's activities. The charming fashion show, presented equally by boys and girls in the Easter term of 1983, is an example of the new activities which coeducation can bring. So was a most successful barn dance and fancy dress disco. Music and drama have been given a shot in the arm by coeducation. Common room life has greatly gained from the increasing numbers of female staff. The whole atmosphere of modern K.C. is more relaxed, gentle and spontaneous than it used to be, though the dominance of the social scene makes school societies more difficult to run, than ever.

The fact remains, however, that K.C. remains a boys' school, with girls in it. In the autumn term 1983 – the time of writing – out of 575 pupils 174 are girls. Out of 52 staff 12 are women. All the boarding houses are presided over by housemasters, except for Wesley, where Ruth and Paul Sorenson are in joint charge. The ethos is predominantly male. Whether the school stays like this or whether it becomes a fully coeducational boarding school, based on equality between the sexes, both among staff and pupils, is a decision which will eventually have to be taken. If the school moves finally in that direction – and the logic of events would seem to dictate that it should – it will be just one more important change in a long history of changes.

References

1 (*16*) Now 62 Whitstable Road.

2 (*16*) The house is called 'a small farm house on the opposite side of Blean Road from Hoathe Court' by a contemporary whose memoir is reproduced in the *Jubilee Book*.

3 (*16*) This is written not in 1985, but in 1891, and shows how quickly nostalgia grows. Accounts of similar whole holidays occur throughout the 1890s.

4 (*17*) The house was demolished in the 1970s to make way for two modern houses. It stood on the corner of Neal's Place Road, where it joins the Whitstable Road opposite St Edmund's School.

5 (*17*) I am grateful to Mrs Bateman of Armidale, 1 Lovell Road, Rough Common, for drawing my attention to a paper by the late P.W. Richards called *Benefits Forgot*, which describes Pillow's history in some detail.

6 (*17*) *C.O.S.* The Clergy Orphans' School was the name originally borne by our neighbour St Edmund's School. The tradition of snowball fights between the two schools still continues.

7 (*32*) I am indebted for these facts to Professor Theo Barker of the London School of Economics, until recently a Governor of K.C.

8 (*34*) Mrs. Peter Rowe, whose husband was Headmaster of Cranbrook School when Mrs Moyle was writing. Today, Peter is on the staff of K.C.

9 (*51*) According to W.L. Blackshaw, this was done with the help of a bicycle pump.

10 (*51*) The situation in the main building remains the same today.

11 (*54*) On the other side of St Edmund's fields, now on University land.

12 (*54*) In the middle of Pine Woods, and a favourite destination for Sunday afternoon walks.

13 (*54*) Schubert's 'Marche Militaire', beloved of the school orchestra.

153

14 *(54)*   A certain N. Harris created a minor sensation when he wore a suit costing twelve guineas, then a trememdous amount of money.

15 *(54)*   Friday evening suppers consisted of a tray of doughnuts, carried round the schoolroom by the unfortunate prefect on duty.

 16 *(54)*   The Dean of Canterbury presented the prizes at Speech Day in 1926 and, as a result, a prize was offered for the best essay on Deans. This was won by John Kitchin, a later Governor of the School.

17 *(54)*   Worn by prefects on Sundays and other important occasions.

18 *(55)*   Mr. Blackshaw has let me see his copy of this remarkable memorial of playground hockey and football leagues, fought out in front of enthusiastic crowds in 1928-29.

19 *(64)*   The story of the short period in which the school changed its name has been recorded by Derek Seager (K.C. 1932-9) in his paper, 'The Year that Wasn't'. His father, a Governor at the time, was influential in persuading his colleagues to revert to the original name.

20 *(66)*   Similar attempts to create School Councils were made in the 'sixties and 'seventies, and another is starting as I go to press.

21 *(67)*   Next year Viscount Runciman acted as the Government's special envoy to the Czechs at the time of the Munich Crisis.

22 *(67)*   Fortunately the school was due to break up on the following Tuesday, so that the day needed only to be put back by 24 hours.

23 *(71)*   W.L. White, who taught Latin from 1931-4

24 *(102)*   Freddie Fowler

25 *(102)*   David Spencer

26 *(102)*   Martin Cox is a K.C. Sixth-former as I write.

27 *(107)*   The 1962 Inspectors had proposed the creation of four senior houses of 45 boarders and the retention of Lower School for boarders aged 11 to 13.

28 *(108)*   The Inspectors picked up the most impressive statistic of all – one in three of those taking 'A' Levels in 1962 had failed the Eleven-plus.

29 *(00)*   It is being revived as I go to press.

30 *(138)*   Memory is deceptive and I thought I would call in aid figures kept at my request by the three housemasters of the senior houses during a typical week in the autumn term of 1982. During the week of 9-16 October the bell rang on average 230 times in each house.

Index

Numbers in **bold** print refer to black and white photographs

Canterbury 25-6, 35, 37, 53, 56, 91, 96-7, 122, 134
St Thomas' Hill, Canterbury 25, 91
Sanatorium (sickness) 39, 93-4, 133-6
Sandon, Dr Nick, memoir of 123-4
Sangster, Dr Paul 30, 121, 130-1, 147-9, **62**
Science teaching 32, 36, 63, 81, 88, 98, 101, 121
School Certificate of Education 46, 81, 83
School Council 60, 66, 108, 132, 154
School House 115
School Room 56, 60, 62-4, **12, 28**
Scott, Arthur 15-16
Scouts 41, 43, 45, 107, 120-2, 139, **18-19, 20, 52**
Seager, Derek 154; memoir of 70-2
Seager, Walter 65, 70
Simon Langton Grammar Schools, Canterbury 53, 61, 74
Sir Roger Manwood's School, Sandwich 61, 83
Sixth Form 48, 60, 62-3, 65, 81-2, 84, 87, 94, 96, 101, 104, 106-7, 109-10, 116, 127, 134, 140, 150
Skinner, H.W. 29 memoir of 49
Slater, Adrian P.L. 11, 100-1, 119, 123 memoir of 91-8
Slump (1929-34) 47, 64
Smallpage, J. Headmaster 20-2, 27, 32
Societies, school 23, 23, 29, 45-6, 63, 82, 89, 108, 126-7, 150
Sorenson, Paul and Ruth 151
Speech Days 46, 59, 65, 76, 80, 82, 85, 87, 91, 93, 98, 104, 109, 111, 126, 136, 141, 154
Spencer David ('Sparks') 75, 83, 87, 91, 93, 98, 102, 154
Spicer, Sydney ('Spic') 53-4, 70-1, 74-5, 78-9, 81-2, 92, 97, 100, 105, 119, **48**
Sport (*see also separate Sports*) 23-4, 30-1, 38-9, 45, 47, 49, 91, 94--5, 101, 103, 106, 135
Stacey, C.D., memoir of 79
Staff, turnover of 22, 38, 105
State Scholarships at 'A' Level 83, 87
Stephens 'C.V.' 93, 100, 105, 119, 123

Strikes, effects of 40, 46, 109
Study-bedrooms 134, 142
Suffolk, C.H.C., memoir of 51
Sundays, customs of 57, 62
Sutherland, Don 93, 140, 149
Swimming bath 46, 68, 91, **25, 46-7**

Tennis, lawn 60, 67, 71, 82, 150
Thwaite, Walton 92, 105, 119
Tremorvah, Truro 68-9, 74-5, 76, 77, 79-80
Trotman, John 111, 149
Truro School 13, 28, 38, 61, 66, 68-9, 74-9, 80-2, 87, 91, 111, 132
Tuckshop 69, 90, 133, **44**
Tulse Hill Hockey Club 47, 83
Tyler, Edward, memoir of 131-3

University entrance and honours at 53, 87, 94, 108

Vernon Holme 80-1, 82, 86-7, 99, 116, 125, 129
Virginian, Old Virginian Club 54

Wallis, Jack 44, 53, 72, 82, 92
Want, Ron 93, 99, **67**
War, First World, K.C. during 40-4, 47, 49-52, 56, 76
War, Second World, K.C. during 61, 68-9, 74-9
Water, K.C. on mains 46, 51
Watson, Barry, memoir of 69-70
Wesley House 60, 84, 112, 116, 129-30, 144-6, 151
Westminster College 64, 65
White, Douglas 70-1, 74, 77, 81-3, 90, 92, 100, 103, 105, 109, 119, 123
White, Peter 93, 113, 119
Whitstable 13, 16-17
Whitstable Road 23, 35, 52, 60, 65, 80, 130, 147, 153
Wicks, Roger 131, 149, **64**
Winter, J.B. 128 memoir of 52-4
Women Teachers at K.C. 43, 50, 81, 144-6, 150
Woodhouse Grove School 14, 22, 28, 30
Woodroffe, Eric 93, 107, 113-14, 131, 138, 142